R33 CONTROL CAR.

20 Signalling Flags

ELECTRICAL APPARATUS.

21 Telephone Control Board
22 Bomb Release Control Board
23 Telephone Battery
24 Bomb Release Battery
25 Aldis Lamp Fuses.
26 Dean Horn Signalling Keys
27 Thermometer for Gasbag Temperature
28 Chart Table Lamp
29 Car Lights (4 in number.)
30 Aldis Signalling Lamp.
31 Distributing Board.

32 Directional Wireless.
33 Wireless Cabinet

THE AGE OF THE
AIRSHIP

THE AGE OF THE
AIRSHIP

Edward Horton

Henry Regnery Company
Chicago

Previous pages: An S.S. (Submarine Scout)
non-rigid airship, one of the Royal
Navy's weapons for combating the
U-boat menace during the First World
War. The gondola is what it appears to
be: an aircraft fuselage

Opposite: A Zeppelin crosses the Rhine
near the Hohenzollern Bridge in Cologne
Overleaf: Immediately after her maiden
flight the *Hindenburg* was pressed into
service as a Nazi showpiece

Designed by Paul Watkins

Picture research by Annie Watt

First published in Great Britain in 1973
Copyright © 1973 by Edward Horton
and Sidgwick and Jackson Limited

Library of Congress Card Number 73-6464

Filmsetting by Typesetting Services Ltd, Glasgow
Printed by Les Presses Saint-Augustin s.a., Bruges
for Henry Regnery Company, Chicago

CONTENTS

PREFACE

IN July 1944 the United States Eighth Air Force rained destruction on a small town bordering Lake Constance in southern Germany. The town was Friedrichshafen and the target was the production facilities of the old Zeppelin organization, at that time engaged in armament work. As the enormous hangars crumbled before the onslaught, the last forlorn dream of the commercial airship perished with them—or so it appeared. For the names Friedrichshafen and Zeppelin were inextricably bound up with that dream: a grand vision of global travel in a mode both elegant and secure. The aeroplane had taken its final revenge on an old rival.

Today, when people think of airships at all it is with much the same sort of feeling that is evoked by dinosaurs: awesome creatures from a long time past, magnificent in their way but inevitable losers in the process of natural selection. Had the end not come with the *Hindenburg* catastrophe at Lakehurst it would surely have come in some other guise, and probably sooner rather than later. In any case, whatever its past glories, the airship is as dead as the dodo.

The purpose here is not so much to challenge this widespread conviction as to recount the story of one of man's most ambitious quests, the easily forgotten 'other' approach to manned flight: the lighter-than-air principle. It begins in the final years of the *ancien régime*, with Montgolfier and Charles and their spectacular balloons. But no sooner had men managed to get into the air than they became frustrated by the balloon's limitations: the inability to control its speed and direction—to be dirigible. For more than a century the sporadic efforts of a host of aeronauts met with little success, and for one intractable reason. There did not exist a suitable means of propulsion. But with the invention of the gasoline-powered internal combustion engine the way suddenly became clear, and controlled flight became a reality.

It is easy with hindsight to say that the path followed by the Wright brothers was the true vision, and that followed by Count Zeppelin misguided, and that in consequence any chronicle of the airship's development is a record of error compounded. Perhaps so. Perhaps the astounding success of the *Graf Zeppelin* is merely the exception that proves the rule. On the other hand the growing interest in the prospects of cargo-carrying airships—not by romantics but by hard-headed businessmen—may indicate that the principle is sound, and the airship's earlier failure means no more than that it was ahead of its time, that it was developed under conditions that could not provide it with a fair trial.

This is conjecture, and the brief age of the airship may be only a fascinating anomaly in the history of transportation. But from either perspective, the past or the future, it provides a splendid tribute to human imagination.

1 LIGHTER THAN AIR

A Monsieur de Faujac de S^t.

EXPÉRIENCE AÉROSTATIQUE *Faite à Versailles le 19. Septembre 1783. en présence de*
avec un Ballon de 57. Pieds de hauteur, sur 41. de diamêtre

Fond, de Plusieurs Accadémies

s Majestés, de la Famille Royale et de plus de 130. milles Spectateurs Par Mrs de Montgolfier

THERE can be few more commonplace observations than that smoke rises, and this does not appear to have any earth-shattering implications. Yet on a June morning in 1783 the people of Annonay, some forty miles south of Lyons, had every reason to think differently. Directly over them an enormous hollow ball ascended majestically towards the heavens; an erroneous theory was 'proved'; the age of flight had begun.

This flying globe, the original balloon, was the inspiration of a middle-aged paper manufacturer, Joseph Montgolfier, who, with his younger brother Etienne, had become fascinated by the possibility of flight. This obsession with flying was by no means unique in his age, but what was singular about Joseph Montgolfier was the way his mind conceived the problems involved. He appeared to start from the seemingly irrelevant point that clouds hang suspended in the air. Why? What was this strange vapour that could perform such a feat? And perhaps if some cloud-like vapour could be enclosed in a lightweight bag then the vapour would lift the bag?

It is churlish to withhold the term genius from a man who could get out of a blind alley like this, not by turning back but by forging straight ahead. There has been much conjecture about what happened next—perhaps it is true that he saw an empty paper bag shoot from his hearth up the chimney—but the lifting power of whatever it was that came off the top of a fire suddenly struck him with the force of revelation. The visual resemblance between cloud and smoke dovetailed sweetly with this startling discovery.

A few experiments with smoke-filled paper bags confirmed the theory in every particular, and the brothers promptly set about preparing a large model for public display. Constructed of linen with a paper lining, this prototype balloon stretched over a hundred feet in circumference, with a capacity of more than 20,000 cubic feet. As a large and incredulous throng packed the market place at Annonay early on the morning of 5 June, the acrid smell of burning straw and wool clippings filled the air. (The Montgolfiers had laboured hard to find the ideal ingredients for producing the best sort of smoke.) The empty fabric, suspended over the fire, rapidly grew into an almost perfect globe. The release order was given and the balloon shot into the sky, where it rose to something between three and six thousand feet and then drifted south, coming to ground ten minutes later, unharmed, in a field a mile and a half away.

The Montgolfiers' balloon became an overnight and world-wide sensation, and when a few months later they repeated their triumph the setting was Versailles, and the enthusiastic onlookers included King Louis XVI and Marie-Antoinette.

Still, like Columbus with his 'Indies', the brothers persisted in their belief that it was the smoke, or at least some vapour released by the fire—'Montgolfier's gas' it was called—that

Previous pages: Versailles, 19 September 1783: the King and Queen are among the spectators as the Montgolfier balloon—carrying a sheep, a cock, and a duck—runs before the wind

Right: Two months later another Montgolfier balloon performs the first manned free-flight. Far right: Professor Charles lands after his first flight, 1 December 1783. Below: Three months earlier his prototype—an unmanned balloon—had suffered at the hands of terrified Gonesse villagers

caused the balloon to rise. The true and simple principle of their hot-air balloon eluded them: air expands when it is heated, its volume increases, and therefore any given volume weighs something less than the equivalent amount of unheated air; in effect, it becomes 'lighter than air'.

By the time of the autumn launch at Versailles, however, a great deal of the Montgolfiers' thunder had been stolen, and by a vastly superior type of balloon altogether.

As soon as word of the Annonay ascent reached his ears, the eminent physicist J. A. C. Charles realized that the means for making a practical balloon had been to hand for several years. Not without reason he was puzzled by the nature of 'Montgolfier's gas', but from the reports it appeared that whatever it was, it was about one and a half times lighter than air. Hydrogen gas, the 'inflammable air' discovered by Henry Cavendish in 1766, was known to be more than fourteen times lighter than air. Indeed Joseph Montgolfier himself had toyed with the use of hydrogen before stumbling on to hot air, but the porous nature of his paper balloon had allowed the gas to escape, and he had abandoned the notion.

Charles saw clearly that all he had to do was put together an envelope that was hydrogen-tight; ascent would then be automatic. Backed by the Academy of Sciences, he promptly engaged the talented Robert brothers, who were known to have concocted some sort of rubber solution. This solution was spread over the silk Charles had chosen for the fabric, forming an envelope only twelve feet in diameter with a capacity just under 1,000 cubic feet.

A public demonstration was set for 27 August, from the Champ de Mars in Paris, and aside from the extremely awkward business of getting the hydrogen into the envelope—the gas was made on the spot by pouring acid over iron filings—the ascent went off without a hitch. The balloon itself, however, fared badly. When it floated down to earth in a field fifteen miles away, the terrified peasantry set about it with pitchforks, and by the time Charles got there it was reduced to shreds and tatters.

The achievements of the Montgolfiers and Charles touched off a wave of 'balloonomania', as Horace Walpole described it, and within a couple of years ascents in both types of balloon were fairly common. The rivalry between the two principles was not resolved as quickly as one might expect—indeed a Montgolfier balloon added the first manned ascent to its other first—but the superiority of the hydrogen type was obvious. It is a tribute to the soundness of the Charles–Robert design that the prototype embraced all the essentials of the hydrogen balloon as it is known today.

Those who pursue ballooning as a sport well know the ecstasy pioneer aeronauts experienced in freeing themselves temporarily from earthly shackles; for the rest it is easy to imagine. It is also easy to understand why it was that as the means and the skills of vertical control were mastered, the total inability to influence horizontal direction and speed—to be dirigible—became increasingly frustrating. Ballast could be jettisoned to gain altitude, gas released to lose it. Aside from that the aeronaut was hostage to the elements. He could neither steer nor go one jot faster or slower than the wind dictated.

This intolerable handicap was attacked boldly right from the beginning. Mechanical wings flailed the air, oars swiped it, weird parasol contraptions snapped open and shut; all to no avail. There could be no propulsion without an adequate source of power, and it was to be some time before one existed. In fact the span of time between that first ascent at Annonay and the first controlled, powered flight was greater than that between the triumphs at Kitty Hawk and Cape Kennedy.

On 24 September 1852, in dead calm conditions, an unwieldy-looking tapered bag filled with coal gas lumbered into the sky over the Paris Hippodrome. From a gondola suspended forty feet below the envelope Henri Giffard kept a watchful eye on a belching 350-pound steam engine, while immediately behind a three-bladed propeller churned the air. Slowly this elongated balloon traversed the city, at between five and six miles per hour, before landing safely, seventeen miles from the point of departure. It was the first dirigible flight.

Trailing smoke from its coal-fired steam engine, Giffard's airship becomes the first dirigible gasbag. But with a speed of only 6 m.p.h. it could not make headway against even a slight wind

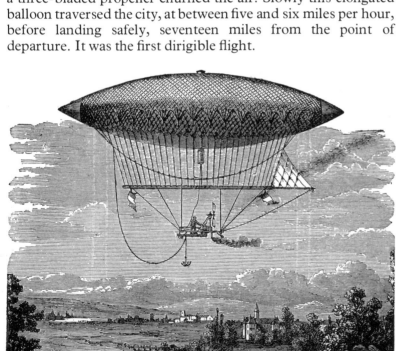

L. GUIGUET.

Several years before his success with steam, Giffard was involved in the notorious *Eagle* project. Absurdly conceived (it was oar-powered) and shamelessly promoted, the *Eagle* was supposed to herald the beginning of a European air service. Not surprisingly, it proved a total—and costly—fiasco

NATION FETE
WILL BE GIVEN, EMBRACING AN
Afternoon & Evening Gala
COMBINED.

UNPRECEDENTED ATTRACTION!
Exhibition of the French Aerial Ship, "The Eagle."
Mr. GREEN's 207th Ascent in his New Balloon.
Concert, Illuminations, and Fireworks.

ONE SHILLING.
THE WONDER OF THE DAY, THE
AERIAL SHIP
By permission of COUNT LENNOX, will be exhibited all the Afternoon. This wonderful
Machine will make its FIRST ASCENT in England from VAUXHALL GARDENS,
during the present Month.

Mr. GREEN will ASCEND for the 207th time in his
NEW BALLOON,
At Five o'Clock. The present occasion will afford an opportunity of comparing the
FRENCH AERIAL SHIP with Mr. GREEN's English Balloon.

A Concert, in Two Acts, in an
And a constant succession of Entertainments   hestra,
Nine in the Even   Day till

Splendid Ex   orks,
And

European Aeronautical Society.

FIRST AERIAL SHIP
THE EAGLE,
160 feet long, 50 feet high, 40 feet wide.
MANNED BY A CREW OF 17,
Constructed for establishing direct Communications between the several
CAPITALS OF EUROPE.
The First Experiment of this New System of
Aerial Navigation.
WILL BE MADE FROM
London to Paris and Back again.
viewed from Six in the Morning till Dusk in the Dock Yard of the Society,
ensington, Victoria Road, facing Kensington Gardens, be-
Hyde Park Corner and the avenue to Kensington
1s.

Henri Giffard was perhaps the foremost designer of steam engines in mid-century Europe. He had also been in touch with the world of aeronautics for a considerable time: almost twenty years before he had had a hand in building an oar-powered monstrosity, the promoters of which had enjoyed considerable financial backing in the anticipation of a regular London–Paris service. Following the collapse of this scheme Giffard appears to have turned away from aeronautics, but his interest was rekindled years later by the growing realization that steam might overcome the old stumbling block of an adequate power source, that is if he could keep the weight of the engine within reason. In the event he managed to get 3 horsepower out of a 350-pound engine which, while extremely inefficient by later internal combustion standards, proved just enough to drive the 143-foot airship forwards. But since he could make only six miles per hour in conditions of almost utter calm, it was obvious to him that even moderate winds would render the craft helpless. In theory a larger envelope would accommodate a bigger and more powerful engine, and this was the path Giffard followed until he ran out of money trying to build a gigantic envelope two and a half times as long as the mighty *Hindenburg*.

Oddly enough the years following Giffard's successful powered flight did not witness a spate of similar attempts, and while balloons were used for observation purposes during the American Civil War the following decade, interest in lighter-than-air flight for practical rather than recreational purposes declined. It was not until the Franco-Prussian conflict of 1870 that the merit of even non-dirigible balloons received dramatic vindication. During the Siege of Paris in the winter of 1870–1 something over sixty balloons braved the encircling Prussian armies, transporting passengers, mail, and even carrier pigeons. This celebrated air lift carried an obvious implication: if free balloons could be so useful, dirigible balloons would be invaluable.

Immediately after the war Paul Haenlein, an Austrian engineer, set to work on a revolutionary solution to the power problem. Ten years before the war the Frenchman Etienne Lenoir had developed a gas engine based on a principle not dissimilar to the later internal combustion engine. A mixture of gas and air, fed into a cylinder, was ignited by an electric spark. Haenlein showed great ingenuity in the way he adapted this engine to the peculiar conditions of an airship. Rather than fill the envelope with hydrogen, he chose the heavier coal gas because it could double as fuel for the engine. He then inserted a smaller balloon—or ballonet—inside the envelope which could be pumped up with air during flight to compensate for the coal gas burned as fuel, thereby preserving the envelope's shape.

The Haenlein airship, which was tested towards the end of 1872, was a failure, and it failed for the same reason that

Both the Tissandier airship (right and below) and Renard and Krebs' *La France* (above) were powered by electric motors. Similar in concept, the two craft differed markedly in performance. The Tissandier brothers managed only 3 m.p.h.: Renard and Krebs averaged 13 m.p.h. during a 5-mile return flight

Giffard's was only a partial success: the engine was too heavy for the lift provided by the gas, and this was exacerbated in Haenlein's case by the need to employ coal gas rather than hydrogen.

The quest for a source of power now turned towards electricity, and as so often in the history of aeronautics France was again in the vanguard. Following a splendid public success with a model, Albert and Gaston Tissandier built a ninety-two foot elongated balloon powered by a Siemens electric motor. To develop a mere $1\frac{1}{2}$ horsepower they needed twenty-four heavy batteries, which gave them a power-to-weight ratio even worse than Giffard's, and while in September 1883 they managed a flight lasting over an hour, the speed was an unpromising three miles per hour.

At Chalais-Meudon on the afternoon of 9 August 1884, two French army engineers, Charles Renard and Arthur Krebs, boarded the most sophisticated airship yet built. Christened *La France* it had a cigar-shaped envelope 170 feet long with a capacity of 66,000 cubic feet; attached to the underside of the envelope was a gondola just over 100 feet in length, which imparted a certain rigidity to the entire structure (the prototype semi-rigid dirigible); at the front of this was a four-bladed propellor screw which would in effect pull rather than push the craft through the air; most important of all it boasted an electric motor capable of developing $8\frac{1}{2}$ horsepower.

The maiden flight was a startling success. Although Renard and Krebs kept *La France* in the air for under half an hour, and covered only five miles, they broke the greatest remaining barrier to controlled flight. For their journey was a round trip, the return half against a fair breeze. And they managed a quite respectable thirteen miles per hour.

By a remarkable coincidence, the very year of this triumph for the electric motor witnessed the arrival of a power source that would render it obsolete for such purposes almost overnight: Daimler's gasoline-powered engine. Light, powerful, and reliable, the gasoline engine was the answer to an aeronaut's prayers, although paradoxically its first applications to lighter-than-air craft were anything but auspicious. Following a reasonably successful trial with a very small gasoline-powered airship, the German aeronaut Woelfert received the backing of the Kaiser for a full-size model, which was completed and ready for trial by June 1897. Although the ship was sound in concept and construction, the designer made the fatal mistake of placing the engine far too close to the envelope. Moments after ascending from the grounds of the Prussian Balloon Corps at Tempelhof in the presence of a large crowd, it burst into flames, exploded, and plunged to the ground, killing both Woelfert and his engineer.

A few months later Tempelhof witnessed a second disaster. The first rigid aluminium-hulled airship, designed by the

Santos-Dumont poses in the gondola of his prototype airship, *Number 1*. Despite an abortive maiden flight, and a near-disastrous second, the airship was judged a success; her owner became a celebrity

Austrian David Schwartz and built under the watchful eye of his wife following his death, crashed in ruins as the result of a slight mechanical fault compounded by pilot error. The pilot escaped with his life, but this costly failure coming so quickly after the Woelfert tragedy bred considerable distrust of the gasoline engine, at least in the context of airships. Indeed from the modern perspective it could be argued that what both airship and engine badly needed at this juncture was a burst of public relations. If so they were in luck.

Alberto Santos-Dumont is the most colourful and perhaps the most enigmatic figure in the history of aeronautics. Born in 1873 into a wealthy Brazilian family—his father had made a fortune in coffee—he showed early evidence of the strong blend of practicality and romanticism that would rule his life: he had a phenomenal aptitude for all things mechanical and a passion for the stories of Jules Verne. And when, blessed with the advantages of a private income, he arrived in Paris at the age of eighteen, he presented an odd and strangely contradictory appearance. He was self assured, dapper, even dandyish, and if he showed no interest in women he seemed eager to savour the other delights of *la belle époque*. At the same time he was unusually self-contained, he could be aloof to the point of curtness, and within a narrow range of interests he was obsessive. He had come to Paris to continue his studies, and, more to the point, he had come in the mistaken belief that dirigible flight was in an advanced stage, and that the land of Montgolfier, Charles, and Giffard would naturally be the centre of this fascinating activity. This delusion, apparently the result of growing up in a remote place and of not distinguishing too carefully between fact and fiction in what he read, was rudely shattered on his arrival. It was widely believed in French aeronautical circles that Renard and Krebs had developed the airship concept to its limit, and interest in the subject was waning. As for Daimler's newfangled gasoline engine, which was noisy, smelly, and probably dangerous, the Germans were welcome to it!

Over the next few years, while he continued his studies and amused himself with one of the first motor cars seen in the streets of Paris, Santos-Dumont appeared to lose interest in aeronautics, or at any rate he did nothing about it. Then in 1897 he came across a recently published book by Lachambre and Machuron, two French balloonists who had assisted the Swedish scientist Salomen August Andrée in the preparations for his ill-fated polar flight the previous year. The *Eagle,* a free-flight balloon hopefully made dirigible by the addition of sails, had disappeared with its crew of three soon after leaving Spitzbergen en route for the Bering Straits, some 2,300 miles distant across the North Pole. No trace had been found, nor would be found until 1930 when a party of Norwegian scientists were to stumble across the remains of the expedition on White Island, 150 miles from the point of departure. (Some exposed photographic film was recovered and provides a fascinating record of the disaster.)

For some reason this story galvanized the Brazilian into action, and he immediately hired Machuron to take him up in a balloon. This first flight—characteristically, Santos-Dumont took along a first-class lunch, complete with champagne and liqueurs—made an overwhelming impression on him, and if he had been slow to make this start he was not slow to follow it up. He promptly designed his own balloon, very small but durable, and became expert in its use. Furthermore his years of experience with the motor car had convinced him of the soundness of the gasoline engine, and regardless of 'expert' opinion to the contrary, he saw no reason why such an engine would not provide the answer to controlled flight. He therefore designed a cylindrical envelope which, although small by airship standards, was perfectly adequate to carry one small man and a light engine. It was 82½ feet in length, with a capacity of 6,400 cubic feet. As for an engine, he simply lifted the one from his De Dion tricycle, modified it slightly for its new role, and finished up with a power plant capable of developing 3½ horsepower for a weight of 66 pounds.

The Jardin d'Acclimatation in the Bois de Boulogne was chosen for the maiden flight of *Number 1*, as the airship was simply named, and on 18 September 1898 Santos-Dumont settled himself into the tiny wicker basket suspended from the envelope, and gave the order to cast off the ropes. Close by stood his sceptical motoring and aeronautical friends, convinced for the most part that the combination of hydrogen gasbag and gasoline engine was suicidal. Unfortunately, they did not confine themselves to forebodings. They could not resist the temptation to give advice, and this was one of the extremely rare occasions on which Santos-Dumont allowed the judgement of others to overrule his own. His almost unerring instinct for such matters had been to take off *into* the wind, but of course this was contrary to all accepted ballooning practice, and when his colleagues saw what he had in mind they inundated him with such a weight of argument that he yielded. The ropes were cast off, *Number 1* rose slowly and hurried downwind straight into a clump of trees at the end of the field. It was an uninjured but very angry Santos-Dumont that scrambled back to earth.

Happily, the airship suffered little damage, and two days later his critics were suitably confounded as they watched it move off steadily into a light breeze, clear the trees effortlessly, and soar out over the Bois de Boulogne. Santos-Dumont now began to experiment with his controls. He shifted the ballast backwards and forwards and *Number 1* dutifully rose and dipped; he moved the rudder and the ship responded at once, turning to starboard;

he brought her right around and then completed a figure of eight, and by now the crowd was cheering wildly. Not even Renard and Krebs in *La France* had demonstrated anything like this ease and assurance of control. Gaining confidence by the moment, Santos-Dumont turned his back on the woods and headed out over the rooftops of Paris, maintaining an altitude of about 1,300 feet. Then he abruptly changed his mind—he intimated later that the steeples and chimneypots had unnerved him—and turned back towards the Bois de Boulogne, giving up altitude in preparation for landing. Suddenly and without warning he was in desperate trouble. The envelope began to sag badly in the middle and then to jack-knife. What had happened was that a considerable quantity of hydrogen had been valved off at the higher altitude, and now that the ship was dropping the remaining gas was contracting. This of course had been foreseen, and there was an air pump whose sole function was to make good the loss of hydrogen and maintain the shape of the envelope. Santos-Dumont guessed correctly that the pump had failed, but there was no corrective action he could take. If he jettisoned what remained of his ballast he would surely rise, the hydrogen would expand, and the envelope regain its shape, but then when he tried to descend again exactly the same thing would happen. There was little point in postponing the ordeal, and the pilot stood helpless as his stricken ship began to drop faster and faster towards the trees below.

As would soon become general knowledge, Santos-Dumont was the very coolest of men in a crisis. With the ground, and almost certain death, rushing up to meet him, he spotted some boys playing down below. As his 200-foot trail rope touched the ground he shouted at them to grab it and run into the wind. The boys, mercifully quick-witted, did as commanded, and by dragging the crippled ship around into the wind increased its lift dramatically. Seconds later *Number 1* crash-landed with little damage to herself and none at all to her commander.

This flight, which was rightly judged a success, launched the personable young Brazilian on the road to world fame, while at the same time it demonstrated convincingly that the future of aviation would be inextricably bound up with the internal combustion engine. 'Le petit Santos', as he became affectionately known, continued to dazzle the Parisians over the next few years with a succession of flights and a steady stream of improved dirigibles, many of them made by the simple expedient of cannibalizing the old for the new. He constructed fourteen in all, but it was not so much the airships as the manner of their flying that so captivated Paris and finally the world.

In 1900 Paris was host to a great international exposition, and to coincide with this Henri Deutsch de la Meurthe, a wealthy industralist and member of the Paris Aero Club, offered a prize of 100,000 francs for successfully flying the seven miles from

Saint-Cloud round the Eiffel Tower and back, in less than thirty minutes. Santos-Dumont leapt at the challenge—which really seemed to be aimed at him alone as he was the only aeronaut with any immediate chance of performing the feat—and set about constructing *Number 5*. This new airship, which was completed the following year, incorporated several notable advances over any of his earlier models, in particular a sixty-foot long wooden keel suspended under the envelope. The triangular keel supported the small wicker basket, or car, as well as a new four-cylinder 12-horsepower engine.

The attempt was set for dawn on 13 July 1901, and at 6.30 *Number 5* was airborne. With a stiff wind behind him Santos-Dumont rounded the Tower in ten minutes, and as he headed back over the Seine it seemed certain that he would make it with time to spare. But he was now flying into the teeth of an increasingly stiff wind, and the thirty minutes ended with *Number 5* still creeping towards the outskirts of Saint-Cloud. Then, the prize having slipped from his grasp, Santos-Dumont found himself in all kinds of difficulty. The engine stopped running and he was immediately drifting out of control, back the way he had come. With his usual presence of mind he began to release hydrogen at the same time as he was struggling to

'Le petit Santos' was famed almost as much for his stylishness as for his aeronautical skill. Blessed with a natural flair for publicity, the young Brazilian was lionized by Parisian society and idolized by the public

The Deutsch prize presented Santos-Dumont with his greatest challenge: 100,000 francs for flying from Saint-Cloud to the Eiffel Tower and back in under half an hour. Twice he failed—and failed spectacularly. Then on 19 October 1901 he rose from Saint-Cloud (opposite), rounded the Tower, and, 29 minutes later, flew triumphantly over the heads of the judges.

Inset: Santos-Dumont at the controls of one of his many airships

23

restart the engine. This meant that should he fail to get the engine going he would at least come down before getting out over the rooftops of Paris. He was still wrestling with the engine when the ship settled into a large chestnut tree in the grounds of Edmund de Rothschild. And there, high in the branches, his rescuers found him half an hour later, nonchalantly eating a fine lunch which the Comtesse d'Eu, Rothschild's neighbour, had thoughtfully sent up to him. Not surprisingly this implausible finale did the aeronaut's reputation far more good than the failure did harm.

Number 5 emerged from the accident with remarkably little damage, and Santos-Dumont was ready for another attempt by 8 August. This time, again with a strong tailwind, the Eiffel Tower was circled even more quickly than before. But now Santos-Dumont had far more serious things to contend with than merely the expected headwind. A faulty valve had been leaking hydrogen for several minutes, and the envelope was beginning to sag ominously, although he still reckoned he had a good chance of making Saint-Cloud. A moment later he was fighting for his life. In the nick of time he had spotted one of the suspension wires, slacked because of the loss of hydrogen, dragging almost on top of the whirling propeller. If he left the engine running the wire would certainly be sliced through, and that could easily touch off a chain reaction of structural collapse that would cut the keel—and the basket in which he was standing—free from the envelope and send it hurtling to the streets below. He stopped the engine, and the ship, still losing gas and now out of control, began losing altitude rapidly, at the same time drifting back towards the Seine and the Tower. Santos-Dumont was obviously hoping for the river, but he had no say left in the matter. With a tremendous explosion *Number 5* smashed into the roof of a hotel in the Trocadéro district. Minutes later firemen plucked her owner from the precarious safety of a window ledge six storeys above the ground. He was unhurt.

If Santos-Dumont was famous before he was legendary now, and he found himself the object of the sort of mass adulation that later generations of film stars and popular musicians would experience. Young men aped his highly stylized appearance, the immaculate pin-stripe suits, high collar, and bowler hat, the moustache, the strangely accented voice, the precise and rather nervous quickness of movement. Women named their sons after him and men their drinks.

It was therefore in an atmosphere of frenzied excitement that a hastily constructed *Number 6* arrived at Saint-Cloud. At 2.42 p.m. on 19 October the signal was given and the airship, virtually the twin of *Number 5*, set off rapidly towards Paris. Once again there was a considerable tailwind and the Tower was rounded in less than ten minutes. And once again Santos-Dumont ran straight into difficulty. The engine cut out, and he had to make the familiar dash back along the narrow keel to try and right it. This time he succeeded, and *Number 6* slowly picked up speed, but he had lost minutes that he could ill afford. Seconds after 3.11 he passed over the heads of the assembled Aero Club judges, circled once, and landed just before 3.13. Had he won or not? Some of the judges said 'yes', because he had covered the distance in just under thirty minutes; others said 'no', because the elapsed time from take-off to landing was just over the limit. The jubilant spectators were in no doubt. 'Le petit Santos' had finally done it. The judges agreed, by a narrow majority, and the prize was his. He grandly divided the money between his workmen and the Parisian poor.

A few years later the Brazilian was to turn his attention to heavier-than-air flight, but in the meantime he continued to delight his adoring Parisians with an almost endless series of exhibitions. *Number 9*, his smallest but finest creation, became one of the prime attractions of the city. With superb control he would navigate from his hangar to his private house, to a dinner engagement at a country house—or at a restaurant in the Champs Elysées. It was pure showmanship, of course, but underlying it was a firm conviction that the small airship had a great potential for personal transport, a claim that would later be made for the helicopter. In fact, even as *Number 9* was skimming over the boulevards of Paris the future of the airship had been grasped by firmer hands.

Number 9 was the finest expression of Santos-Dumont's belief in the airship's future—as a means of private transportation. Small, manoeuvrable, and reliable, she soon became a familiar sight in the Paris sky

BIRTH OF THE ZEPPELIN

Previous pages: Count Ferdinand von Zeppelin and his first airship. *LZ1* (photographed over Lake Constance on 2 July 1900) was badly under-powered, yet she had many of the features that would soon make Zeppelin the foremost name in airships

O N July 1900 Ferdinand von Zeppelin celebrated his sixty-second birthday. The rather short, bald, heavily moustached old man might also have been celebrating the beginning of his life's work had it been more auspicious. Six days before, an enormous sausage-shaped gasbag, with Count Zeppelin at the controls and four others on board, had shambled into the air to spend just over seventeen minutes wandering about over Lake Constance. While this first trial of the first Zeppelin was not an outright failure, it hardly appeared to be a landmark in the history of aviation. Yet for all her ungainliness *Luftschiff Zeppelin Number 1*, or more simply *LZ1*, had provided the thousands of spectators lining the shores of Lake Constance with a glimpse of the future. From that day forward the Zeppelin vision was to dominate the entire course of airship development.

The ageing Count had come to aeronautics by a curious route. He had been a career soldier most of his life, serving with distinction in the Austro-Prussian and Franco-Prussian wars, and eventually attaining the rank of Brigadier-General. Then in 1889 he had foolishly crossed swords with the War Ministry, and even worse with the young Kaiser himself, over a political matter. He was retired from the army the following year. Therefore, at the age of fifty-two, he was free to devote himself to a problem that had been nagging him for many years: the application of balloons and airships to modern warfare.

In the United States during the Civil War, where he had been acting as German observer, Zeppelin had seen reconnaissance balloons in operation, and he had managed to make one ascent. Then again he had followed closely the spectacular employment of balloons during the Siege of Paris, and years later the widely-reported flights of *La France* had caused him considerable alarm lest Germany be left behind in developments which struck him as having obvious military implications. So it was that towards the end of his military career he had begun agitating for measures to remove this danger. Ironically, by dismissing this rather troublesome officer the army was adopting the best measure imaginable.

LZ1 was the second airship Zeppelin designed, although she was the first one actually built. A commission set up by the War Ministry had rejected plans for an earlier model, for sound enough reasons, but as a consequence, government help was not forthcoming for his new design, which was a great improvement. It was therefore with some private backing but mainly with the bulk of his own personal fortune that he set to work in a huge pontoon shed moored near Friedrichshafen, on the north shore of Lake Constance. What distinguished this airship from all other pioneer craft was her truly monstrous size. She was 420 feet long, nearly forty feet in diameter, and had a capacity of 400,000 cubic feet—more than sixty times that of Santos-Dumont's *Number 1*. Furthermore this great volume of

hydrogen gas was not merely pumped into a large gasbag; rather it was divided among seventeen individual compartments, all held together by a sturdy aluminium framework consisting of transverse rings and longitudinal girders, the whole braced by diagonal wiring and covered with fabric. Each of the two gondolas suspended beneath the hull contained a 15 horsepower Daimler engine, while from a catwalk running between the gondolas a weighted cable was suspended, with the intention that it be slid forward or aft to effect vertical control.

Altogether it was a very impressive piece of work, except that, as was amply demonstrated on that first flight, it was wildly optimistic to expect two small engines to power over ten tons of airship successfully. And the second trial in October of the same year merely confirmed this. The young economist Hugo Eckener, who was covering the event for a Frankfurt paper, stated the self-evident truth that an airship capable of only 13–16 miles per hour was inoperable in conditions of moderate wind.

With his airship written off as a flop and his company's funds exhausted, Zeppelin might have been expected to retire from the field. On the contrary he ransacked his own already depleted coffers, raised a large sum from a far-sighted aluminium manufacturer, and for the rest persuaded the King of Württemberg to let him run a lottery!

Hugo Eckener (right) first came to Count Zeppelin's attention when he reported unfavourably on *LZ1*'s second flight. Yet within a few years Eckener had become the airship's most effective champion, and Zeppelin had found the ideal collaborator and successor

This second Zeppelin was very similar to the first, with the important difference that the more advanced engines developed 65 horsepower each. But despite this very significant improvement, *LZ2* had a brief and unhappy life. Her first trial, at the end of November 1905, nearly ended in disaster when engine failure during the launch caused the tail to smash heavily into the water. The damage was repaired by the new year, and on 17 January *LZ2* made her one and only flight. Some twenty miles from Friedrichshafen engine failure once again necessitated a crash-landing, and while Zeppelin managed this admirably, savage storms that night destroyed the airship as she lay at her makeshift moorings.

Zeppelin was temporarily crushed by this latest misfortune—according to Eckener he vowed to give up altogether—but soon he was back in business, having once again managed to scrape together the substantial amount of money required for a new project; *LZ3*, almost identical to her predecessor, was put together with astonishing speed, and underwent her first trial on 9 October 1906. She performed beautifully, flying effortlessly into a stiff wind and responding well to every touch of the controls (elevator surfaces had been introduced with *LZ2*, replacing the clumsy sliding weights, and new stabilizers were fixed on to the stern with the rudder placed between them). Zeppelin gave a repeat performance the next day, and suddenly all Germany—including the Kaiser—was aware that the rather quirky old Count and his huge dirigibles were to be taken seriously. He received a large grant from a government agency, and the army stated its willingness to buy one from him, providing it came up to rigid specifications; with this encourage-

ment he set to work on yet another airship. *LZ4* was the largest
to date, 446 feet long with a capacity in excess of half a million
cubic feet, and she also incorporated new Daimler engines of
105 horsepower. During the summer of 1908 the new ship made
several memorable flights, smashing all existing records for
distance and endurance, and even on one occasion carrying the
King and Queen of Württemburg as passengers.

It was now virtually impossible to dispute the worth of the
giant airship, and all that remained to do before handing it over
to the army was to manage a 24-hour return flight. Count Zeppelin
announced that he would perform this feat on 4 August, and in
the early morning *LZ4*, bearing the Count and ten others, rose
majestically from the calm waters of Lake Constance and began
a triumphant progress westward along the Rhine. The selected
route, from Friedrichshafen to Mainz and back again, had been
well publicized, and factories, shops, and schools along the way
emptied as people poured into the streets to cheer. Eleven
trouble-free hours slid by, and then, ten miles short of Mainz,
the Count's old nemesis struck again. The forward engine
became overheated and he had to make a forced landing for
repairs.

An hour and a half later *LZ4* was in the air again, circling
Mainz near midnight, and then turning back southward. For
almost a hundred miles the airship droned steadily over the
sleeping German countryside, and then the forward motor failed
again. While it might have been possible to reach the safety of
Lake Constance on the one remaining engine it was risky, and
Zeppelin wanted to take no chances on this crucial journey.
He immediately altered course for the Daimler works at
Stuttgart, where permanent repairs could be made, and shortly
after daylight *LZ4* came to rest in a field just outside the village
of Echterdingen, close by the factory. The hastily summoned
Daimler mechanics had almost finished their repairs when a

sudden, violent thunderstorm broke over the scene, wrenching some of the mooring ropes from the hands of the ground crew. *LZ4* pitched and yawed, shot 600 feet in the air and then came smashing down on to a tree and disappeared in a sheet of flames.

Much has been made of the storybook sequel to this tragedy, and to a later age it may seem quite incredible. Within hours of this seemingly final blow to the old man's dreams, money began to pour into the Zeppelin headquarters: large donations and small, contributions from businessmen, from peasants, from municipal corporations, from school children, from seemingly everybody in Germany. It amounted to some six million marks, far more than the Zeppelin company had ever possessed. Cynics might argue that this spontaneous outburst of national generosity had been triggered by the skilful publicity provided by Hugo Eckener, who had long since changed from sceptic to active supporter. It is certainly true that Eckener, who was at Friedrichshafen when word of the disaster came in, lost no time in getting the story out to every newspaper in the country, and he did not scruple to point out what a blow to national prestige the collapse of the Zeppelin enterprise would entail. In any case, it merely confirms the airship's enormous debt to Hugo Eckener.

A rejuvenated Zeppelin now saw his immediate task as satisfying army requirements for an airship fleet. During the next year he rebuilt *LZ3* to bring her up to their specifications and completed two new ships. The first of these, *LZ5*, along with the 'new' *LZ3*, were duly taken over by the army, but *LZ6* was not, because the Prussian Airship Battalion had successfully steered the authorities in the direction of its own semi-rigid designs. Once again the Zeppelin fortunes were on shaky ground, but this time the old man and his company were saved not by fortune, nor by lottery, nor by national sentiment. Rather, Zeppelin allowed himself to be persuaded that the airship had a commercial as well as a military future, and that with his great prestige he was in an ideal position to exploit this. With Eckener as his partner he duly founded the world's first passenger airline in November 1909.

DELAG, the abbreviation by which the Deutsch Luftschiffahrts Aktien Gesellschaft (German Airship Transport Company) was known, went into operation the next year, and soon an expanding network of airship routes reached out to the major German cities. By 1912 several ships were in constant operation, usually with a full complement of twenty passengers. With Eckener having assumed his seemingly inevitable role as Director of Flight Operations, DELAG proceeded in the brief spell before war broke out to establish a performance and safety record that stands any comparison. More than 10,000 passengers completed 107,000 miles during 1,588 flights without suffering so much as a scratch.

This truly remarkable achievement, at a time when other

Much of Eckener's almost legendary skill as an airship captain stemmed from his experience with small sailing boats. His 'nose' for weather was proverbial

advanced nations were struggling through the very earliest stages of airship development, and the passenger aeroplane was scarcely dreamt of, was above all the triumph of Hugo Eckener. This economist turned journalist turned airship captain was superbly equipped for his new role. He was an astute business-man possessing, as has been seen, a natural flair for publicity; he combined the qualities of sound judgement and great prudence with rock-like courage. Furthermore he seemed to be gifted from the beginning with an uncanny aptitude for every aspect of flight control, from training crews to navigation and even weather forecasting. Taking all this in conjunction with his striking physical appearance and forceful personality it is easy to see why an aura of infallibility grew up about him, and it is no exaggeration to say that the confidence inspired by this one man—and this confidence later became world wide—is the most important single element in the development and operation of the passenger airship.

While the German airship industry was making such dramatic strides, what of developments in other countries? Was it possible that in the highly competitive pre-war years Germany's rivals were content to sit back and watch as she added an entirely new dimension to commercial and military life?

It is easy to forget at this point that the German awareness of airships in the early years of the century had not sprung fully grown as a sort of national far-sightedness. It had been foisted on the German people, and a reluctant army, by the dedicated efforts of an eccentric old visionary. If Zeppelin's early struggles had not captured the popular imagination it is extremely unlikely that anything like such great progress would have been made. Furthermore, Zeppelin thought of the airship as a weapon of war, and later as commercial transportation. Both functions required the mammoth dimensions and rigid con-struction of his early creations, and the large rigid airship became accepted as the norm. Britain and France, and for that matter the United States, lacked a Ferdinand von Zeppelin, and therefore the impetus for a concerted airship programme.

France, to be sure, was the natural home of aeronautics, and Santos-Dumont was every bit the hero there that Zeppelin was in Germany. But the cavalier Brazilian had a completely different and fundamentally wrong-headed view of the airship's potential. He saw it as a marvellous plaything for the sporting rich, and possibly in the distant future as an airborne comple-ment to the passenger motor car. If on occasion he expressed enthusiasm or foreboding—depending on his mood—about its military potential, when it came to actually designing another airship he seems never to have given it a thought. So it was that in France, after Santos-Dumont retired from the field, a host of other adventurous individuals continued in the tradition of

The British non-rigid airship, *Beta*, at Firminy near Dunkirk. A far cry from the advanced Zeppelins, *Beta* was nonetheless a useful training ship for pre-war pilots

small, light, non-rigid dirigibles. The French government maintained a stony indifference to the enterprise.

In Britain during the early years things were much the same, although the War Office did show occasional concern at reports coming out of Germany. The first British airship was constructed by the aeronaut Stanley Spencer, who on 19 September 1902 managed to get across London in an hour and forty minutes. The next few years saw the appearance of several more privately built airships, and a number of successful flights—including a Channel crossing by the *City of Cardiff* in 1910.

By this time, however, the War Office had decided to take a hand. Over several years it had been making sporadic and parsimonious handouts to the army balloon factory at Farnborough, and for its pains had received in 1907 a well-designed non-rigid airship modestly entitled *Nulli Secundus*. After her maiden flight, a stately progress from Farnborough across West London, round St Paul's and then to Crystal Palace, the first army dirigible was cannibalized to make the semi-rigid

Nulli Secundus II, which was subsequently dismantled. This was followed by two more, *Beta* and *Gamma*, which performed with only limited success, and while in 1911 an airship company was formed as part of the new Air Battalion of the Royal Engineers—later to become the Royal Flying Corps—it was left to the Royal Navy to attempt the more ambitious project of building a rigid airship along Zeppelin lines.

Rigid Naval Airship Number 1, the *Mayfly* as she was dubbed, was completed by May 1911, and during that summer was subjected to a series of pre-flight tests. All was pronounced satisfactory, and on 24 September the *Mayfly* was being eased out of the hangar for her maiden flight when a sudden wind dashed her sideways against the entrance, crushing her framework so badly that repairs were not attempted. The Admiralty did not think the experiment worth repeating.

In America, early airship development is clearly divided between farce and tragedy. A wealthy adventurer named Walter Wellman arrived in Paris at the beginning of 1906, and,

Nulli Secundus II was a completely rebuilt version of the first British Army dirigible, *Nulli Secundus* ('Second to None'). The new airship made several short hops, but never achieved anything so spectacular as her predecessor's cross-London jaunt on 5 October 1907. *Below*: It was not until 1911 that the first Zeppelin-type airship was constructed in Britain. The Vickers-built *Mayfly* was earmarked for the navy, but never went into service. Here seen during pre-flight trials at Barrow, Lincolnshire, the *Mayfly* was wrecked by an ill-judged wind before she could rise into the air

Left and below: Two views of *Eta*, a non-rigid and the last British airship built under military supervision before the First World War. Launched in August 1913, she could manage 42 m.p.h. with a crew of five. Right: The *America*, about to ditch after Wellman's foolhardy attempt to cross the Atlantic in October 1910. The photograph was taken from the deck of the British rescue vessel

with his appetite whetted by conversations with Santos-Dumont and other aeronautical celebrities, he ordered an airship to be built to his specifications and delivered to Spitzbergen for an attempt on the North Pole. The *America*, as she was named, took off on 2 September 1907 with a crew of four, only to limp back a few hours later, crippled by engine difficulties. Undaunted, Wellman abandoned the Pole for an even more audacious stunt. He carted his airship off to Atlantic City and, without a single trial, set off for Europe. A few hours out to sea the *America* ran into a bad storm, and for the next three days the helpless craft, blown 1,000 miles off course but still scarcely out of sight of land, was spotted by a British warship. The crew was rescued, but the airship was lost, and Wellman mercifully retired from the field.

One member of the expedition, Melvin Vaniman, remained convinced that the scheme was practicable, and the next year he persuaded the Goodyear Tire and Rubber Company to back his design for an extremely large non-rigid (400,000 cubic foot capacity) airship using their newly acquired technique for rubberizing fabric. The *Akron* was a sophisticated airship, and there was no reason in principle why she could not have made the transatlantic crossing. However, Vaniman made the terrible mistake of allowing himself to be hurried with his tests—the venture was arousing a great deal of public interest— and on 2 July 1912 huge crowds lining the Atlantic City harbour witnessed the appalling spectacle of the airship exploding to bits just minutes after rising from her moorings. The explosion may have been caused by faulty gas valves (if gas is not released during the ascent an airship is almost certain to burst under the enormous pressure), but whatever the cause of the disaster, Vaniman and the other three members of the crew perished, and with them American interest in airships, at least for the time being.

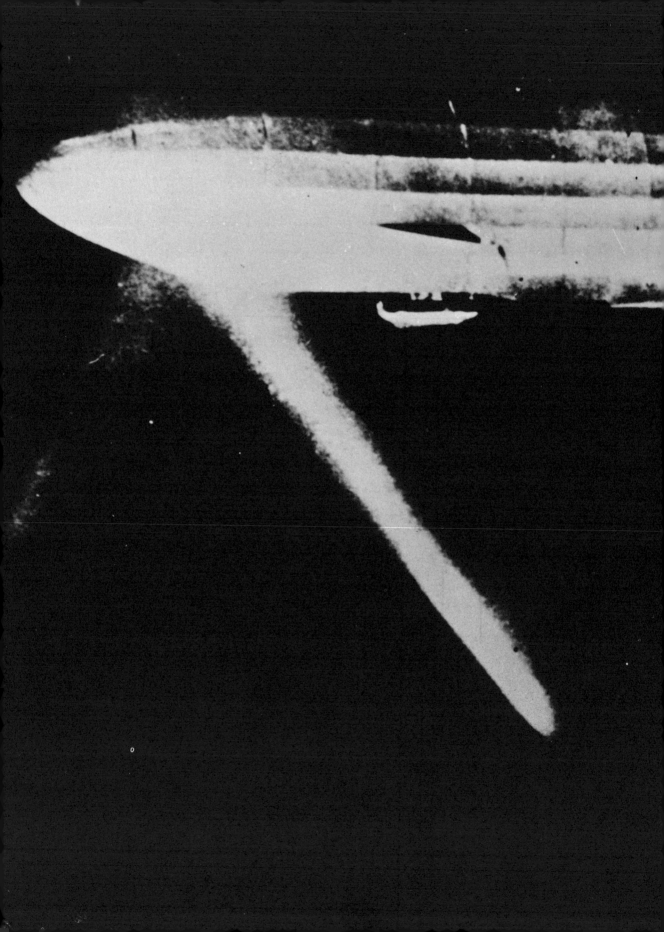

3 WEAPONS OF WAR

WHEN war broke out in the summer of 1914 the armed forces of three of the belligerents, Germany, Great Britain, and France, possessed an airship capability of some sort. So too did Italy, which had not yet joined the fighting, and indeed the Italian army had already made active use of its two non-rigid airships as early as 1912, during the fighting with Turkey. Yet while each of these countries made extensive use of airships during the war, in the popular imagination airships and the First World War conjures up one stark image: Zeppelins in the London sky.

There are several reasons why this is so, the effectiveness of British propaganda not least among them. Indeed while it is impossible to measure such things it is reasonable to say that the carnage resulting from the Zeppelin raids on Britain was nothing compared with the damage done to Germany's reputation by them, particularly in the United States where reports of 'Hun savagery' fell on fertile ground. While the raids certainly did spread considerable death and destruction, their record appears almost insignificant in the light of more recent aerial warfare. During the entire Zeppelin campaign, which extended from the beginning of 1915 to the summer of 1918, the bombs killed 557 people and did an estimated £1,500,000 worth of damage. As Eckener remarked many years later, after a war that had ushered in air power of another dimension, 'They were no more than pin-pricks, painful, but still pin-pricks.' (In the next sentence he goes on to add, 'It was a tragedy of lost opportunity!')

However, the military significance of a weapon is not determined solely by the statistics of destruction. Zeppelins added a new and sinister dimension to warfare, and a people long sheltered from the grim realities of civilian war were horribly alarmed at the sight and the thought of these enormous monsters droning over their heads. The threat was easy to over-estimate, and at least in 1915, when anti-aircraft defences were virtually non-existent, many German strategists as well as London civilians were convinced that it would be decisive. While events would totally disprove this, and indeed the airship would turn out to be far more useful in the undramatic area of sea patrol than in strategic bombing, it looked as though Britain would pay the supreme penalty for having been so slow off the mark in its development.

The German armed forces entered the war with seven Zeppelins, six belonging to the army and one to the navy. As well as these the army possessed one airship manufactured by the rival Schütte-Lanz Company, which differed from the Zeppelin design most notably in its wooden framework. This tiny armada had been assembled during the two preceding years, at a time when DELAG's continued success had convinced the most hardened sceptics that the airship had a vital military role.

Top left: Sketch of a Zeppelin attack on London. Left: Artist's impression of a similar raid on Antwerp. Above: Soldiers, police, and onlookers gather in front of a gutted building after Zeppelins bomb London's East End. Right: *Punch* cartoon of 25 August 1915

THE ACHIEVEMENT.

COUNT ZEPPELIN. "STANDS LONDON WHERE IT DID, MY CHILD?"
THE CHILD. "YES, FATHER; MISSED IT AGAIN."
COUNT ZEPPELIN. "THEN YOU HAD NO SUCCESS?"
THE CHILD. "OH, YES, FATHER; I'VE GOT HOME AGAIN."

As soon as war broke out the three remaining DELAG Zeppelins (*Hansa, Viktoria Luise,* and *Sachsen*) became training ships, and a crash building programme was launched.

Nor was any time wasted in putting the existing airships into service. On the night of 5 August, just two days after the invasion of Belgium got under way, the army Zeppelin *Z6* dropped 420 pounds of artillery shells on Liège, was hit by anti-aircraft fire, and limped back to Germany only to crash over Bonn. The extreme vulnerability of a low-flying airship to concentrated firepower, even from rifles, was demonstrated again and again in the opening weeks of hostilities, and while the losses were soon made good, the German High Command began to favour the idea of shifting the attack from the inferno of the Western Front to the undefended skies over England. By the new year the Imperial Navy's Airship Division, under the able command of Peter Strasser, was ready to strike, and on the morning of 19 January three Zeppelins, *L3, L4,* and *L6,* set off across the North Sea. *L6* was forced to return to base after encountering serious engine trouble, but the other two reached the Norfolk coast late that evening, and succeeded in spreading a fair amount of destruction as well as killing four persons before returning to their base without mishap.

This was the first of a series of forays, really little more than exploratory probes, that continued through the first half of 1915. While they resulted in some damage and quite a few casualties they were but a foretaste of the onslaught to come with the arrival of bigger and better Zeppelins: the million-cubic-foot class that appeared in the summer of 1915. While these new Zeppelins suffered from some of the liabilities of their predecessors— they could only fly in good weather and at night, and then only when there was little or no moonlight; they found extreme difficulty in navigating in the dark and missed their target more often than not—they were in other respects a great improvement. Fitted with four 210-horsepower Maybach engines they could cruise at around fifty miles per hour at a height of 11,500 feet, their range extended the width of England, and they could carry two tons of explosives. Furthermore the Zeppelin factories were speeding up construction, and by the end of the year the army and navy had received ten each of these new types. As well, the Kaiser had finally been persuaded, reluctantly, that London was a legitimate military target. Prior to this he had expressly forbidden bombing attacks outside the docks area, but under great pressure from his military advisers he rescinded these orders in July—saving only royal palaces and buildings of purely historic significance.

Henceforth, the commercial centre of London was the prime target, and on the night of 8 September Heinrich Mathy, commander of the navy's *L13,* demonstrated just how vulnerable a target that could be. *L13* set out for London with two sister ships, but had to complete the mission alone when they both turned back with engine difficulties. At just after 10.30 p.m. bombs and incendiaries smashed into a cluster of textile warehouses behind St Paul's Cathedral. The resulting fire, which gutted an important part of the City, accounted for one-third of the property damage caused by the Zeppelin raids throughout the whole of the war. Then, just five weeks later, during the evening of 13 October, Mathy's *L13* and three other naval Zeppelins converged on London. *L13, L14,* and *L16* all missed their targets—again the City and the docks—although their bombs accounted for many lives, but *L14* cut a swath from the Strand eastward to the City, only barely missing several crowded theatres. The raid left 71 dead and 128 wounded, the highest tally of the war, and had weather conditions allowed this sort of punishment to continue unremittingly it could have assumed a crucial military importance. In fact it was the final raid of 1915.

The following year saw the German airships broaden their attack to include targets as far north as Edinburgh (where their greatest success was the destruction of £44,000 worth of whisky stored in a warehouse), and if London had faced the aerial threat poorly defended, most provincial cities had no defence at all. On the last day of January 1916, a fleet of nine Zeppelins spent

The gondola of the German navy Zeppelin *L6*. With two sister ships, *L6* set out on 19 January 1915 for the first airship raid on the British Isles

TOUR
PRINCIPALI T
AUSTRIA GE

ZEPPELIN

LVG

RUMPLER
TAUBE

DFW

NEMICI

SEG

Top left: The machine gun and look-out position on the outer envelope of a Zeppelin. Left: *L13* (from which the photograph was taken), *L12*, *L10*, and *L11* starting out for England in August 1915. Above: A chart distributed by the Italian Touring Club as an aid to airship and aeroplane identification

In the full glare of
searchlights a Zeppelin
proceeds across central
London. In the early stages
of the campaign Britain's air
defences were so minimal as
to give the giant raiders very
nearly a free hand

the entire night droning over central England searching for the industrial cities, shrouded in the mist below. They did not find what they were looking for, but by the time the last of them headed back out across the North Sea they had left behind seventy dead, and a national uproar over the state of Britain's air defences.

New anti-aircraft batteries were established all over the country, and several squadrons of the Royal Flying Corps were assigned strictly to night flying. At the beginning of May the Royal Navy even mounted an attack, unsuccessful, on Zeppelin hangars at Tondern, on the west coast of Denmark. But the lull that began at this time and continued through the summer had nothing to do with British defences; the Imperial Fleet had turned its attention to other matters (the Battle of Jutland took place on 31 May).

When the assault began anew, in August, it was on a larger scale than ever, and with the mightiest airships yet seen. The new 'super-Zeppelins', as the British named them, were almost twice as large as the previous class, they were a little faster, and they had an operational ceiling of 13,000 feet. On 24 August the first three of these super-Zeppelins, *L30*, *L31*, and *L32*, led a fleet of thirteen airships on southern England, but only one—Mathy again in *L31*—got as far as London, where once again he wreaked considerable havoc, this time in the docks area. Then on 2 September the largest airship armada of the war embarked on what Strasser fondly hoped would be the beginning of the final chapter in the air war: a sustained onslaught that would pound Britain into submission. Ironically, it was the airship, not the enemy, that was tried·and found wanting.

Twelve naval and four army airships converged on south-east England to deliver this *coup de grâce*, but as was so often the case, their numbers began to dwindle long before they reached London. *L17* and *LZ97* were forced back by unfavourable weather, while *LZ98* mistook Gravesend for the London docks, again highlighting the acute problem of night-time navigation; her bombs were released to little effect. Three more raiders drifted far north of their target area and bombed the Midlands, again causing only minimal damage, while over London itself catastrophe overwhelmed the army's new and much vaunted Schütte-Lanz *SL11*. Picked out by searchlights over a northern suburb, the unwary ship was stalked by three R.F.C. fighters, one of which, piloted by Lieutenant William Leefe Robinson, managed to get into position directly above her. Moments after Leefe Robinson unloaded two drums of explosive across her back *SL11* filled the night sky with a ghastly light. The crews of five of the naval airships still moving in to the attack watched horrified as the monstrous inferno plunged to the ground at Cuffley, cremating all on board. The raid, instead of being a mere failure, had become a disaster.

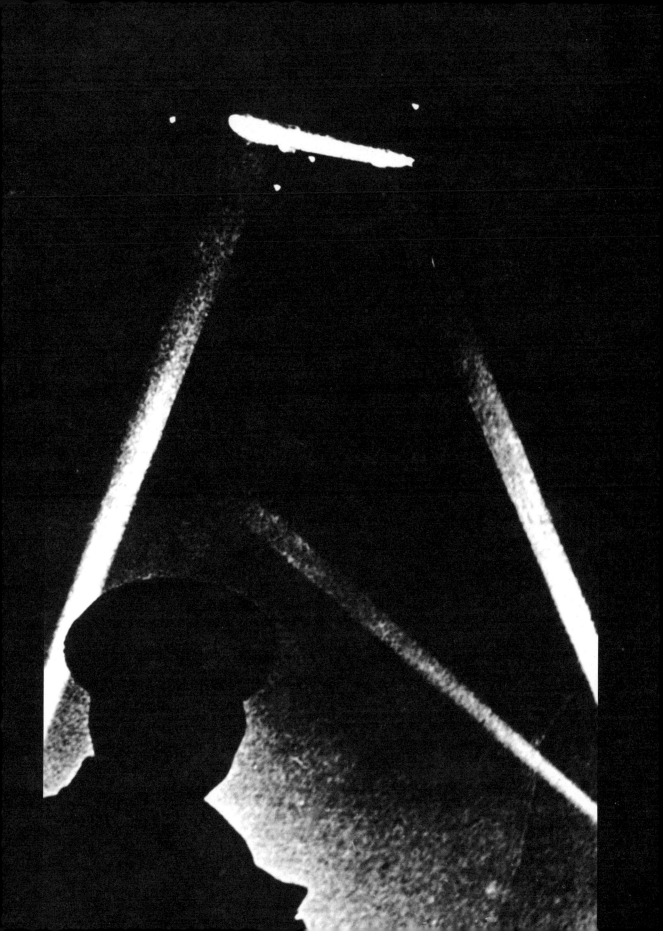

Right: William Leefe
Robinson and the wreckage
of his victim, the
Schütte-Lanz *SL11*. The
spectacular effect of
Zeppelins exploding in the
night sky is shown (above) as
L31, commanded by Heinrich
Mathy, is shot down over
Potters Bar on 1 October
1916. Opposite: *L34*,
commanded by Max Dietrich,
perishes over Hartlepool two
months later. Bottom: A
souvenir photograph album of
the air raids

Overleaf: The gruesome
remains of *L31* on the
morning of 2 October. There
were no survivors here—and
none on *SL11* and *L34*

This was the beginning of the end for the airship offensive against London. The army promptly gave up such raids altogether, and while Strasser refused to follow their example with his naval division, the ensuing months vindicated the army's feeling of disillusion with the strategy. Despite the fact that in succeeding raids only the larger super-Zeppelins were employed, the casualties mounted alarmingly. *L33* and *L32* were brought down on 23 September, and then on 1 October came the most crushing blow of all: the seemingly invincible Mathy perished in the flaming wreckage of *L31*, shot down over Potters Bar. Two months later, during a raid that deliberately gave London a wide berth, *L34* and *L21* were blasted out of the sky.

If Strasser refused to abandon his dream completely, this unbroken string of humiliating defeats began to have a telling effect. Even the new range of Zeppelins that entered the fray in 1917—slightly larger than the *L30* type and with a ceiling of more than 20,000 feet—were unable to cope with the dramatic improvements in Britain's aerial defences. The loss of five of these new Zeppelins during the 'Silent Raid' of 19 October marked the effective end of the campaign, and in a macabre postscript, Strasser himself died in the last futile strike the following August. As a war machine the Zeppelin was as obsolete as the long-bow.

Yet if the autumn of 1917 marked the eclipse of the airship as a strategic bomber, it also witnessed the most astonishing display of the Zeppelin's potential for a quite different role:

Far left: British S.S.-type coastal non-rigid watching over the British fleet in the Mediterranean. The control and engine gondola (left) was a converted aircraft fuselage. Below: Zeppelin *L12* is towed into Ostend after falling victim to British anti-aircraft fire at Dover (August 1915)

Above: German aircraft
triumph over a French
airship. Opposite: A
Zeppelin is pursued by a
French scout. Right: Remnant
of a Zeppelin shot down over
Salonica (now Thessaloníki)
in Greece

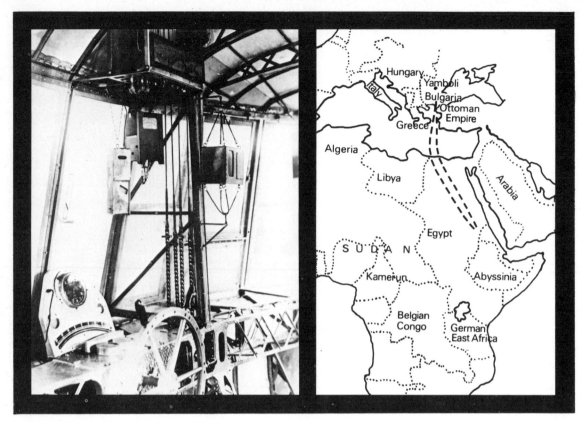

Close-up of the control cabin
of the *L59*, 'The African
Ship', with the route
followed on her epic voyage of
November 1917

intercontinental flight. And while the remarkable journey of
'The African Ship' may have contributed nothing to
Germany's war effort, it added enormously to the prestige of her
airship industry, and to the world-wide interest in lighter-than-
air travel that blossomed during the post-war years.

For three years General von Lettow-Vorbeck had tenaciously
held a grip on German East Africa, in the face of remorseless and
increasing Allied pressure. By the summer of 1917 his position
was desperate. His comparatively small force was completely
cut off from the outside world, surrounded by the enemy, and
very nearly bankrupt of ammunition and medical supplies. Were
his garrison to surrender—and this could not be long delayed—
Germany would end the war with no colonies, an intolerable
state of affairs for a nation that had so recently and so whole-
heartedly entered the ranks of the imperialists. The beleaguered
force must be relieved, and the only possible means of doing this
was by airship.

With Hugo Eckener and another pre-war DELAG
commander, Ernst Lehmann, taking charge of the preparations
for this bold venture, the naval Zeppelin *L59* was hastily rebuilt
to increase her capacity to very nearly $2\frac{1}{2}$ million cubic feet,
the largest yet. On the bitterly cold morning of 21 November
1917, *L59* took off from Yamboli in eastern Bulgaria, the

furthest advanced Zeppelin base. Under the command of Kapitän-leutnant Ludwig Bockholt, *L59* set out across the Sea of Marmara on what was intended to be a 4,300-mile non-stop journey—one way. This latter stipulation, for the twenty-two man crew, must have been ominous, but there was no possibility of refuelling at the journey's end, as gasoline was one of the many things Lettow-Vorbeck needed desperately, and it was certain that the five Maybach engines and whatever fuel remained would be among the most welcome 'cargo'. Indeed the entire airship was to be cannibalized: the engines would power dynamos for the radio transmitter; the cotton envelope would be suitable for clothing; the metal girders would be ideal for constructing a long-range radio tower, a field hospital, dwellings of all sorts; and as a final ingenious touch the catwalks were lined with leather suitable for making boots. On top of all this 'The African Ship' was laden with thirteen tons of medical and military supplies.

All through the daylight hours of the 21st, *L59* moved steadily southward, close to the Aegean shore of Turkey, and as night descended she left the land behind and struck out across the Mediterranean, carefully skirting the island of Cos, where enemy aircraft were reported to be patrolling. After a long and perilous night battling with violent thunderstorms, the ship crossed the shore of Africa near what is now the Egypt–Libya border and headed inland across the Sahara. If the night had been dangerous the day was hardly less so. It was difficult to navigate over a landscape devoid of known landmarks, and to make matters worse the ship was constantly buffeted by currents of hot air rising from the desert below. Moreover the crew, almost all of whom were severely airsick, had to spend the day working constantly to keep the ship from rising to such a height that a fatal quantity of the superheated hydrogen would be valved off.

Night wore on and still the Zeppelin droned on over the Sahara wastes, dead on course and on schedule despite her difficulties. Just after midnight, without warning, a radio message was received ordering the mission to be abandoned. 2,800 miles out from Yamboli—beyond Khartoum—*L59* was simply to turn around and come home. A false report, long after attributed to British Intelligence, had been received by the German High Command to the effect that Lettow-Vorbeck and his men were now in such a tight net as to make relief impossible, that his surrender was imminent.

Two days later, in the early hours of 25 November, the exhausted and thoroughly disheartened crew nursed their airship down to her Yamboli moorings. In just over ninety-six hours *L59* had covered 4,200 miles, and still had sufficient fuel for another 3,000-odd miles. Although an obvious failure, it was surely the Zeppelin's greatest wartime achievement, and it heralded the rigid airship's true role.

4 OVER OCEAN AND ICE

EVEN months after the armistice, on 21 June 1919, the German fleet interned at Scapa Flow was scuttled by its crews. Two days later most of the surviving naval Zeppelins were destroyed likewise, which was particularly infuriating for the victorious Allies, as they were bent on expropriation.

It appeared certain that this desperate action, and the resentment following in its wake, would spell utter ruin for the German airship industry, but by a curious twist of fate it actually led indirectly to its salvation.

Eckener, in firm control now since the Count had died in 1917, had wasted no time in attempting to shift the Zeppelin Company from a military to a commercial base by reviving DELAG. Indeed by that fateful June day construction work on the first of what was intended to be a brand new passenger fleet was nearly completed. The *Bodensee* commenced trials in August and went into service between Friedrichshafen and Berlin the following month. While small by comparison with the monsters of 1917–18 (she had a capacity of just over 700,000 cubic feet), the *Bodensee* afforded very comfortable accommodation for her passengers, and with a cruising speed of around eighty miles per hour she was nearly twice as fast as her DELAG predecessors. During the last three months of 1919 she transported about four thousand passengers over 32,000 miles in 103 flights. The following year a second new passenger ship, the *Nordstern,* was ready to join her, and it was hoped that as well as reopening all the pre-war DELAG routes the service could be expanded to include other major cities in Europe. The Allied powers, however, had not finished with the Zeppelin Company.

The four naval Zeppelins that had survived June 1919 had already been turned over to the victors (two going to Britain and one each to France and Italy). A fifth (*L72*), that had not been completed in time to be commissioned but was nevertheless adjudged war material was also given to France. Now it was decided to confiscate the two commercial airships as well, on the flimsy pretext that the materials used in them had been manufactured during wartime and for military purposes. *Bodensee* went to Italy and *Nordstern* to France, and if that were not crippling enough substantial compensation was demanded for the naval airships that had been scuttled before they could be shared out among the victors. As a final turn of the screw it was stipulated that any future German airships could not exceed 1,100,000 cubic foot capacity, which effectively ruled them out of the natural next stage in airship development, transoceanic flight. The Zeppelin Company clearly needed another miracle. It came in the shape of a somewhat aggrieved United States Navy.

This airship harvest garnered by the Allies had not gone unnoticed across the Atlantic, and the U.S. Navy was anxious to get its hands on a Zeppelin (although in marked contrast to the

Europeans the Americans were prepared to pay for one, a suggestion that actually increased opposition to the scheme). After considerable wrangling with the Allies, the Americans and Germans came to an agreement whereby the Zeppelin Company was to construct an airship which would be turned over to the United States in lieu of $800,000 compensation. Furthermore, since the navy insisted that the ship should be proved airworthy by transatlantic delivery, the restriction on size was set aside, to be replaced by the stipulation that future German airships must not exceed the capacity of her largest wartime Zeppelins, roughly two-and-a-half million cubic feet. That was all Eckener needed.

LZ126, or *ZR-3* as the American navy designated this, their third rigid airship, was completed towards the end of September 1924. She was, by a slight margin, the largest yet built, 658 feet long, ninety-one feet in diameter, and with a capacity of 2,542,320 cubic feet; five 12-cylinder Maybach engines of 350 horsepower each gave her a top speed of eighty miles per hour. After two trial flights, one of them a lengthy round trip from Friedrichshafen to Malmö, Sweden, Eckener was ready to attempt delivery. On 13 October, the latest—and as far as any-

A rear view of *LZ126* under construction. Built by the Zeppelin Company for the U.S. Navy, she was flown across the Atlantic for delivery, and renamed *Los Angeles*

The British airship *R34* arrives at Pulham after completing the first transatlantic round trip by air (July 1919). Her design was based on that of a captured Zeppelin

one knew, the last—Zeppelin rose slowly from her moorings through the early morning mist, and then set off westward across France in sparkling sunshine. At 4 a.m. on the 16th Boston lay directly below, and daylight found her cruising majestically over the skyscrapers of New York. At 9 a.m., after a flight lasting eighty hours and covering more than 5,000 miles, *ZR-3* landed at Lakehurst, New Jersey.

The far-sighted Eckener was hoping for a lot from this epic journey: not only was it to demonstrate the Zeppelin's enormous potential for transoceanic commerce, it was to dispel some of the anti-German feeling still running high six years after the war. Only in a climate of international goodwill, or at least acceptance, would it be possible to shake off the crippling restraints on Zeppelin construction. He was not disappointed. An enormous, frenzied crowd mobbed the Germans as they quit the airship,

which a few days later was christened *Los Angeles* by President Coolidge's wife. Eckener then set off on a lengthy round of meetings with American businessmen in an attempt to drum up interest in the possibilities of commercial flight. Wherever he went he was greeted with courtesy and his ideas with enthusiasm, and when he set sail for Germany in mid November he could congratulate himself on every count. The American people saw him as a personal friend and as the embodiment of the new, peaceful Germany; and they described his airship with superlatives.

American goodwill was one thing; the arduous business of resurrecting the German airship industry quite another. The Allied strictures remained, the Zeppelin Company was without funds, and there was little enthusiasm for Eckener's grandiose schemes in German official quarters, where the attention had turned to heavier-than-air flight. Once again the rigid airship appeared to be on the verge of extinction, at least in its homeland. For whatever Eckener's difficulties, in other quarters the Zeppelin principle was being exploited with considerable enthusiasm and some success, and it could be only a matter of time before German pre-eminence was lost.

In Britain there had been, in the last years of the war, a belated attempt to bridge the painful gap in airship development, but while extensive and very valuable service was performed by naval blimps, the few rigid airships completed before the Armistice made no impact at all. But the determination to assemble an impressive military fleet did not die with the war, and in 1919 three new rigid airships entered service. The first of these, *R32*, was used for little more than training, but *R33* and *R34*, both closely patterned along the lines of a 'super-Zeppelin' that had been forced down on English soil in 1916, immediately thrust Britain to the forefront of airship development. For not

R33, twin to *R34*, was successfully used to launch small aeroplanes during flight Overleaf: *R34* flies over Nelson's Column; to the right, Major G. H. Scott, commander of *R34*

only did they look like Zeppelins, they actually performed like them, and if *R33* gave the longer service it was left to her sister ship to perform the most spectacular flight to date.

In the spring of 1919 the London *Daily Mail* offered a prize of £10,000 for the first non-stop flight across the Atlantic, and, in a blaze of international publicity, aviators from both sides of the ocean began feverish preparations for the assault. A U.S. Navy blimp managed the thousand miles from Long Island to Newfoundland, but after she was wrenched from her moorings to drift off in the right direction, crewless, the contest quickly boiled down to a race between several British military aeroplanes based at Newfoundland and the newly commissioned *R34*, moored in Scotland. The victory and the prize went to Alcock and Brown for their brave achievement in a Vickers–Vimy bomber, but two weeks later the world's attention was riveted on the giant airship as she glided away from East Fortune, shortly after midnight on 2 July. Whereas the Vickets–Vimy bomber had barely managed to stagger to a crash-landing in an Irish bog,

Wreckage of the British-built
R38 at the mouth of the
Humber. There were only five
survivors of what was
intended to be a final trial
before the airship was
handed over to the U.S. Navy

after surviving the most hair-raising perils, *R34* crossed the
Atlantic with almost complete serenity. Towards the end of the
journey, after Nova Scotia had been reached, she had to weather
severe storms and a threatened fuel shortage, but in the early
afternoon of 6 July, after 108 hours and twelve minutes in the air,
R34 touched down at an airfield outside New York. A week
later she was safely moored at Pulham, Norfolk, having
completed the first transatlantic round-trip by air.

The British airship industry, in its new-found confidence,
could now look forward to an ambitious future in which its own
expertise applied to the Zeppelin design would provide a
standard of excellence for others to follow. It was with such high
hopes that work proceeded on the largest airship yet built anywhere, *R38*. This huge British 'Zeppelin', a shade under 700
feet in length with a capacity of 2,750,000 cubic feet, was earmarked for the U.S. Navy, and from the beginning of 1920
right through until construction finished in June 1921, an
American crew was stationed in Britain, undergoing exhaustive
training at Howden Air Base in Yorkshire.

Finally on 23 June *R38*, or *ZR-2* as the Americans
designated her (*ZR-1* was still under construction in the United
States), underwent her first test flight. The results were dis-
appointing, even ominous: for some reason she was difficult to
control. A second trial, five days later, proved similar and the
third flight, on 17 July, was very nearly the last. While the ship
was building up speed the elevator controls failed altogether, and
instead of maintaining an even keel *R38* began to pitch wildly.
Two girders immediately buckled and it was only by a hair's

breadth that disaster was averted, and that Flight Lieutenant Pritchard, the British officer still in command, guided the stricken airship back to a safe mooring.

Despite their growing reservations the Americans were anxious to press forward with the final trials and to take possession of their first rigid airship, and after hasty repairs had been carried out the next flight was set for 23 August. If *R38* performed well this time the hand-over would be completed at last, and the American crew could finally point her in the direction of Lakehurst, New Jersey, where an enormous hangar had been prepared to house both *ZR-1* and *ZR-2*.

Soon after dawn on the 23rd the airship left Howden for the last time, cruised all day over the North Sea and then proceeded south towards Pulham, her final destination before the ocean crossing. As she droned serenely above the English coast it seemed that after her many tribulations *R38* would triumph in the end. She was performing well, she was handling easily, and when it was discovered that heavy fog at Pulham made landing impossible it seemed no more than an opportunity to wait the night out over the North Sea, and then run through some final speed trials the next day. But the fog did not lift in the morning, and by the afternoon it was decided to turn back to Howden. A final high-speed trial was completed along the way, and then as the afternoon drew to a close, the citizens of Hull were treated to the splendid sight of the returning airship manoeuvring gracefully overhead. At 5.37 this vision turned to a waking nightmare as *R38* buckled in the middle, tore herself in two, and plunged straight into the river Humber. Forty-four of the forty-nine men on board perished.

The *R38* disaster—which was attributed to structural weakness under great pressure—very nearly killed British interest in airships, and it would be several years before there was sufficient confidence to launch another project. In the United States, on the other hand, despite the fact that fifteen Americans had died in the tragedy, work went forward on *ZR-1*, and by September 1923 the airship was ready for trials. Christened *Shenandoah*, an Indian word meaning 'Daughter of the Stars', *ZR-1* was, as usual, closely patterned on a captured Zeppelin, with the very important difference that she was the first rigid airship to be inflated with non-flammable helium. The new ship performed admirably, and over the next two years she became a familiar sight all over America, along with the *Los Angeles* which Eckener had delivered in October 1924. The only real snag, the only thing that was holding back an ambitious airship programme, was the fact that the navy possessed only enough helium for one ship, and as a consequence when the *Shenandoah* flew the *Los Angeles* hung deflated in the Lakehurst hangar, and vice versa. The Americans had no intention of using hydrogen, which they considered to be

Two views of the
Shenandoah (*ZR-1*), the
largest airship of her time,
and the first rigid to be
inflated with helium. In
October 1924 she performed a
round-trip flight across the
United States, covering more
than 9,000 miles

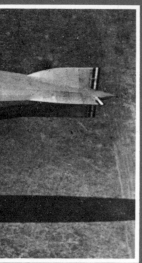

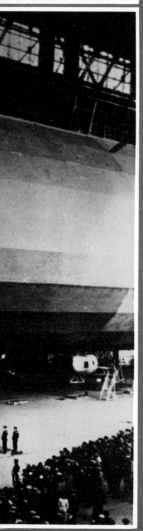

unacceptably dangerous, and with helium as scarce as it then was the airshipmen were stymied. They could do nothing but set up impressive performance records, including a trans-continental round trip by the *Shenandoah* at the very moment that Eckener was guiding the *Los Angeles* (inflated with hydrogen on this delivery flight) across the Atlantic.

By the summer of 1925 enthusiasm for these airships was running high, and there was talk in official quarters of taking the *Shenandoah* across the North Pole. In the event the navy settled on the less ambitious and seemingly less hazardous course of sending her on a trip to the American Midwest. To many, including the *Shenandoah*'s commanding officer, Zachary Lansdowne, it was by no means obvious that a late-summer excursion to the Midwest was any less risky than a full-blooded assault on the Pole. On the contrary, Lansdowne considered such a flight perilous in the extreme because of the sudden and killing storms that wrack the Midwest at that time of year, and he even lodged an official request to postpone the flight.

His protest got him nothing more than a week's delay, which was meaningless, and on the afternoon of 2 September he followed his orders and the 'Daughter of the Stars' rose from Lakehurst and turned to the west. At three o'clock the following morning strong headwinds over Cambridge, Ohio, brought the airship almost to a standstill, while lightning raked the sky away to the north and east. Deviating from his prescribed route as little as possible, Lansdowne turned slightly south to skirt the thunderstorm, but still the headwinds made progress painfully slow. At five o'clock two whirling storm clouds converged to form a line squall directly above the *Shenandoah*, and her fate was sealed. Suddenly she began to rise quickly and no corrective measures had the slightest effect. Under full power and with the nose pointing downwards at an angle of 18 degrees the airship was sucked remorselessly up into the eye of the storm, rising from 2,100 feet to 6,300 feet in minutes. Helium was valved off frantically; the appalling climb was finally arrested, and the now heavy ship began to drop like a stone. The nose was immediately pulled up, all the water ballast was jettisoned, and at 2,600 feet the dive was arrested. An opening in the sky to the south appeared to spell hope, but it was illusory, and after hovering uneasily for a few moments with two of the five engines now out of commission, the helpless airship began to surge upwards again, even faster than the first time. Again the nose was thrust down and the three remaining engines opened wide, and again to no avail. But what was now causing Lansdowne the greatest alarm was the certainty that when the uncontrollable climb finally ended, the ship would fall again, and there was no water ballast left to jettison. In anticipation of this he ordered the crew to prepare for the desperate manoeuvre of cutting loose the fuel tanks, but this last chance never came.

Stretched beyond endurance the *Shenandoah* twisted in one final agony and then began to disintegrate. The control car wrenched free and plunged into the darkness, carrying Lansdowne and seven others to their deaths. Girders snapped like matchsticks as the full fury of the storm tore into the dying airship, and moments later she broke in two, and then the after-section broke in two again. With the surviving crewmen fighting to gain some sort of free-ballooning control, the three fragments drifted to earth and were scattered over the rolling farmlands near the village of Ava. Miraculously, twenty-nine of the thirty-five men outside the control car escaped alive.

The *Shenandoah*'s nightmare did not end there: dishonour followed hard on disaster. Without a moment's grace, waves of looters descended upon the wreckage and began carting off anything and everything that could be prised free; not only stores and provisions, but bits of torn fabric, twisted pieces of framework, mutilated personal possessions. All through the day the pillage continued and by the time darkness came the 'Daughter of the Stars' had been stripped bare.

During these middle twenties the fascination with polar flight was not confined to one section of the U.S. Navy Department. It captured the imagination of adventurers all over the world and, most important, it was becoming an obsession with the foremost explorer of the time, and probably of this century: Roald Amundsen. The Norwegian, whose greatest success had been in reaching the South Pole a month before Captain Scott some thirteen years previously, had made two airborne attempts at the North Pole by the spring of 1925. On both occasions the attempt had been by aeroplane, and now his attention switched to dirigibles.

By a happy chance this coincided almost exactly with the rare appearance of a tested and proven airship for sale, a semi-rigid dirigible designed and built by the Italian airshipman, Colonel Umberto Nobile. *N-1*, while small by the standards of rigid airships (348 feet long, 650,000-cubic-foot capacity), was ideally suited for Amundsen's purpose, and he began negotiating for its purchase. Immediately he ran into diplomatic troubles, a foretaste of things to come, when Mussolini expressed displeasure at the idea of the expedition proceeding under Norwegian command, but a compromise of sorts was finally hammered out. *N-1* would be renamed *Norge* and fly the Norwegian flag, but while Amundsen would command the expedition as a whole, control of the airship would remain in Nobile's hands. With Il Duce's blessing the airship left Italy on 10 April 1926, and began the long trek north to King's Bay, Spitzbergen.

Amundsen was in a hurry because he knew full well that there were plans afoot to beat him to the Pole, and after the briefest of stopovers at Pulham and Oslo the *Norge* pressed on for Leningrad. But there, intolerable weather grounded the expedition for more than two weeks, and when it finally reached King's Bay on 7 May it was to find Commander Richard Byrd there before them, feverishly readying his Fokker monoplane for the final sprint. Two days later, while preparations on the *Norge* were entering their final stages, the blow fell: Byrd and his companion Floyd Bennett circled the airfield triumphantly and touched down after a gruelling sixteen-hour flight in which they claimed to have flown directly over the North Pole—a claim that has subsequently been disputed. Amundsen dutifully offered his congratulations, and in a spirit of some disillusion, the crew of the *Norge* pressed forward to the start. Just after nine o'clock on the morning of the 11th the airship, with sixteen men—and Nobile's dog—on board, rose above King's Bay and set out across the immense and frightening wastes of the Polar Sea. Throughout the long and sometimes foggy arctic day the *Norge* closed on her destination, and at 1.30 a.m. on the 12th, with the broken ice floes clearly visible below, the navigator Riiser-Larsen announced their arrival at the North Pole. Amundsen dropped a weighted Norwegian flag, followed by the Stars and Stripes from Lincoln Ellsworth, a wealthy American whose financial backing had made the expedition possible; Nobile completed the ceremony with the flag of Italy.

The really awesome portion of the journey now lay ahead, for Amundsen had never conceived of this as a mere dash to the Pole. He was determined to cross the unexplored wastes between there and Alaska, to fly right over the top of the world, and as the early morning wore on the *Norge* plunged into the unknown and into rapidly deteriorating weather. The fog was heavy, and, worse, it was freezing and the ship was becoming

The *Norge*, which became the
first airship to cross the
North Pole in May 1926. The
achievement was marred by
the bitter and public row
between the airship captain,
Nobile, and the expedition
commander, Amundsen

covered in ice. There was no visibility and the radio was useless because the aerial was ice-coated, making navigation pure guesswork, and the crew was exhausted at the very time that it was vital it be alert to the slightest danger. This grave situation continued throughout the 12th, until finally in the early hours of the 13th the weather began to clear; at 6.30 in the morning land was sighted and Riiser-Larsen's hasty calculations showed they were approaching the northernmost tip of Alaska, Point Barrow, which meant that they had flown more or less blind for twenty-four hours and yet had stayed dead on course. The landfall was gained an hour later, and as though with a new lease of life the airship and her fatigued crew continued down the coast towards Nome, the final destination. But early on the morning of the 14th, after a storm-wracked and again foggy night, Nobile and Amundsen agreed that a landing could be delayed no longer. They knew they had been lucky to survive the night, weaving a tortuous path between, and finally in desperation above, the towering coastal mountains, and they were no longer certain where they were.

It no longer mattered; any reasonable landing site and some sign of humanity would be gratefully accepted. At 7.30 a.m. after more than seventy hours in the air, the *Norge* touched down softly outside the tiny community of Teller, Alaska. Nome was only fifty-five miles away to the south.

The voyage of the *Norge* was a great triumph for the airship and equally a triumph for Amundsen and Nobile; and it is sad that to a large extent this was overshadowed by the furious public row that soon broke out between the two men over whose was the greater credit. The reputations of both suffered by this petulant display, and as an enraged Nobile stormed off for home with Amundsen's denunciations ringing in his ears it could have been taken as a portent of the level to which international co-operation was sinking.

Nobile arrived in Italy to a hero's welcome, which was naturally exaggerated since the dispute with Amundsen was bound up with national pride. His overriding concern now was to build another airship as quickly as possible and launch a truly Italian polar expedition, and he might well have thought that the public adulation boded well for his plans; if so, he reckoned without Mussolini. One can almost sympathize with the vainglorious dictator as he tried to juggle the nation's prestige with his own: Nobile's triumph bore such splendid witness to the renewed grandeur of Rome; but it was unendurable for the man who was, after all, the living embodiment of those Roman virtues to have to share even a little of the limelight. Mussolini refused permission for the project.

The following year events conspired to force a painful reconsideration. In May 1927 Charles Lindbergh became the

most famous airman of his and doubtless any time by flying alone in the *Spirit of St Louis* from New York to Paris. Clearly there were endless new triumphs in store, and it was unthinkable that Italy should not capture her share of the glory. At the same time, the citizens of Milan were putting together a subscription to enable Nobile to realize his dream, and it would be churlish and certainly unpopular to dampen such enthusiasm. Mussolini bowed to the inevitable, and work immediately began on a new airship. The *Italia*, an improved version of the *Norge*, roughly the same size but with greater lifting power, was completed by March 1928, and was safely moored at King's Bay in early May. The long journey north had been a hazardous one, accomplished in the teeth of weather conditions every bit as bad as anything the arctic wastes could be expected to provide, and it was with considerable optimism that Nobile and the other members of the expedition set about the final preparations.

The programme was considerably more ambitious than a mere flight across the Pole, every bit the equal of the long and perilous journey to Alaska. Nobile intended to explore Nicholas II Land, about which virtually nothing was known, and he wanted to chart some of the extreme northern Canadian coastline and a large, unexplored region of Greenland. After a false start on the morning of 11 May, when dreadful weather conditions forced the airship back to the relative safety of her moorings, the expedition faced a stark reality. It was snowing heavily and without relief, and despite frantic attempts to sweep the *Italia* clean, the snow was building up across her back. Nobile realized that at some point the structure would take no more and would simply buckle, but there was nothing he could do as he watched his men slowly lose ground to the deepening snow. Finally the weather cleared, the snow melted, then froze to solid ice as the temperature suddenly dropped then melted again, and the *Italia* dried out. Luckily she emerged from the ordeal unscathed, and in the early afternoon of 15 May she struck out once more for Nicholas II Land. The *Italia* was carrying sixteen men, including two scientists and a newspaper-man, again Nobile's dog, a wealth of scientific equipment, and more than four thousand miles worth of fuel. Sixty-nine hours later she returned to King's Bay bearing a detailed survey of some fifteen thousand square miles of land that had hitherto been uncharted.

With the difficult part of the undertaking behind him, Nobile now pressed ahead with his plans to reach the Pole, indeed to visit the Pole: the *Italia* had been especially prepared to withstand a descent on to the icefloes. Just before 4.30 on the morning of 23 May the last journey of the *Italia* got under way. Twenty hours later, shortly after midnight, the North Pole lay below them, flags and a cross were dropped, observations taken, and radio messages dispatched to the Pope, the King of Italy, and of course Mussolini. Disappointingly, weather conditions made the landing impossible, and after hovering expectantly over the target for a couple of hours Nobile decided to turn back for King's Bay.

Through heavy and freezing fog the *Italia* inched slowly southward, very slowly because she was fighting headwinds of gale force. The wind and the fog conspired to make accurate navigation impossible, and after thirty exhausting hours there could no longer be any pretence that Nobile or anyone else knew where they were; their one brief radio

exchange with the base had given them no clue as to their position, and the only thing that was certain was that they were nowhere near King's Bay. Nor could anything be done about the ice that was steadily building up on the ship's exterior surface. At 9.25 a.m. on the 25th Nobile faced an emergency. The elevators jammed and it was necessary to stop the engines in order to repair them. At this point Nobile committed a terrible blunder. He allowed the airship, which was now floating like a free balloon, to rise above the fog, above the clouds, and into brilliant sunshine. She was bound to rise like this in the absence of controlled power because she was 'light' after burning such a weight of fuel, and by the time the engines were started again the *Italia* had soared to 3,000 feet. While it was a pleasant relief to leave the fog behind it was hardly an aid to navigation to be completely out of touch with the surface, and Nobile was obliged to descend through the fog once again. The *Italia* was now doomed. At the higher altitude a great deal of hydrogen had been automatically released to equalize the pressure between the expanding gas and the decreasing atmospheric pressure. That in itself might not have proved fatal, but the hot sunshine had warmed and therefore further expanded the hydrogen, causing yet more to blow off through the valves. Now as the ship came down into the cooler and denser air the hydrogen rapidly contracted, and its volume decreased to such an extent that it was unable to lift the weight of the ship, or to check her from falling further. Had Nobile been quick enough to realize this danger he could have released hydrogen the moment the engines were shut down, not nearly as much hydrogen as was eventually lost, but just enough to keep the floating airship from rising appreciably. As it was, a desperate last-minute attempt to lighten the ship by throwing overboard all ballast and indeed just about everything within reach, proved fruitless; the *Italia* sank helplessly towards the ice. There was a sickening crash, and the control car burst open spilling Nobile, his dog, eight of his colleagues, and a merciful quantity of equipment on to the ice. Before they could scramble to their feet to secure the wreck, the *Italia* lurched into the air again, as if grateful to be relieved of so much weight. With six crewmen still aboard she disappeared from view forever.

The survivors appeared to be little better off. Nobile was in great pain from a broken arm and broken leg, and if the others were less badly injured they were all suffering to some degree from shock. As they gathered their scattered provisions and equipment together they could not avoid the awful realization that they were utterly lost. There was only one small ray of hope. A radio set was salvaged—intact—and the operator, Guiseppi Biagi, lost no time in putting together a makeshift antenna and sending out a distress signal. There was no reply, and the men huddled together in the one four-man tent that had 'landed' with them. Nobile at any rate was simply preparing himself for death.

The S.O.S. message had, however, been heard at King's Bay, or at least enough of it had been heard to connect the distress call with the deafening silence from the *Italia*. Within a day a massive air search was under way, but with no further radio contact—Biagi tried repeatedly but did not get through—the rescuers faced a hopeless task; how could they know where to look? Tantalizingly, the stranded men's radio was working perfectly, and they listened with mounting despair to cheerful messages and improbable theories as to their whereabouts.

The days crawled by, the meagre rations stretched thinner and thinner, and, if possible, the situation was being made worse by the knowledge that the ice pack was drifting steadily south-east, taking them further and further from the area that the searchers were likely to cover. After a week, it was decided that three of the party should strike out across the ice to the nearest land and somehow try to reach help. The others waited, the monotony broken only by Biagi's unanswered transmissions and increasingly gloomy bulletins describing the fruitless search. There was no real hope left on either side when on 9 June, the sixteenth day adrift, King's Bay picked up a faint message—and this time they got Biagi's position. The lost expedition went wild with delight as the evening broadcast told them that help was on the way. But their ordeal was not yet at an end.

The continued drift, which was difficult to measure accurately, managed to keep them just outside the net as the rescue aircraft—there were ten in all—criss-crossed back and forth over the new search area. Two more weeks went by before they were finally spotted, and the following day, 24 June, Nobile was evacuated. But when the Swedish pilot who flew him out returned for the next load he was grounded by engine trouble, and found himself imprisoned with the others. It was not until 12 July that the last man was lifted from the ice pack—the same day that a Russian ice-breaker accidently stumbled across two of the men who had set out for help. Their companion, the Swedish scientist Malmgren, had died weeks before.

While it was rightly considered a miracle of survival that only one of the nine men originally marooned on the ice perished in the ordeal, the death roll did not end there. Rescue missions to the Arctic are notoriously dangerous, and given the number and the type of aircraft involved, it is unremarkable that one of these aeroplanes was lost. On 17 June the French *Latham*, with six men aboard, vanished on its way to King's Bay to join in the hunt. It carried the one man Nobile believed would be able to find them: Roald Amundsen.

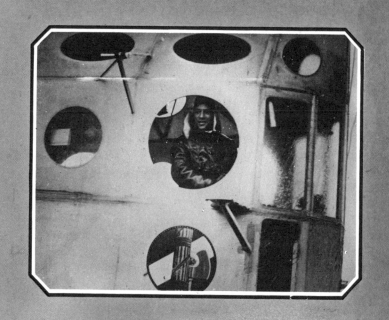

5 TRIUMPH AND TRAGEDY

Previous pages: The
Hindenburg in flames over
Lakehurst, New Jersey

Opposite: An ageing Hugo
Eckener gazes down from the
Graf Zeppelin

DURING the long weeks that the *Italia* expedition
hovered between life and death, work was entering its
final stages on the airship which would immediately
eclipse all rivals, and go on to become not only the most famous
airship but very likely the best-known conveyance ever. For
Hugo Eckener had not admitted defeat when he returned to
Germany in 1924, much fêted but empty-handed, and the
world was about to see the result of his determination in the
long cigar shape of the *Graf Zeppelin*.

Eckener, it will be recalled, was confronted by two obstacles
to his plans for developing a transoceanic air service, both of
them seemingly insurmountable: German airships were limited
by international agreement to a size that made long-distance
journeys with a heavy payload—passenger or freight—impossible; and the German government considered the aeroplane,
not the airship, to hold the key to an airborne future. The first
obstacle evaporated the following year when Locarno Pact
removed the restrictions on Germany's airship industry. That
meant there was nothing standing in Eckener's way but money,
and like his late mentor he was a past master at raising
money. In the grand Zeppelin tradition he tried to get
permission to run a lottery, and when this was refused, he
turned directly to the German people. As he admitted himself,
it was quite a different matter to campaign for funds rather
than merely to ride on the wave of national sympathy, but the
plight of the Zeppelin Company was every bit as grim as it
had been after the Echterdingen disaster of 1908. The
'Zeppelin–Eckener Subscription' was launched, and during
1925 and 1926 Eckener and several other members of the
Zeppelin organization devoted all their energies to a most
exhausting lecture tour. Not surprisingly, Eckener found the
whole business distasteful, but he persisted, and finally when
the donations totalled three-quarters of the target (some
£400,000), the German government stepped in with the
balance.

Eckener now had the money to build the sort of airship he
wanted, but he did not have the hangar to build it in, and
he could not afford both. What he had in mind was something
like the later *Hindenburg*, a true luxury liner, 'an airship in
which one would not merely fly, but would also be able to
voyage'. With great reluctance Eckener was forced to set his
sights a little lower, although many who flew as passengers on
the *Graf Zeppelin* would argue that she fell little short of the
ideal. This most successful of airships was fast, comfortable,
and provided most of the amenities of civilized living. If she
appeared spartan by comparison with the finest ocean liners of
her time she appears luxurious by comparison with the best
that commercial aviation can provide in ours. Above all, the
Graf Zeppelin satisfied the most important criterion for any

One of the most extraordinary of all airship photographs: the *Graf Zeppelin* flies low over Wembley Stadium during the 1930 Cup Final. Those in the back row seem torn between the two spectacles

transporter of human cargo: she was superbly well constructed.

Her vital statistics were impressive enough. Despite the physical limitations on size dictated by the dimensions of the Friedrichshafen hangar she was by far the largest airship constructed to date: 775 feet long, 100 feet in diameter at the widest point, and 3,707,550 cubic feet in capacity; she was powered by five Maybach engines of 530 horsepower each, which gave her a cruising speed of more than seventy miles per hour. The gondola, affixed to the belly of the envelope near the nose, comprised a control room with a navigation area partitioned off from it, and behind that a radio room and a fully equipped kitchen, a fairly spacious lounge that doubled as dining saloon, and ten two-berth staterooms. The crew's quarters were, as usual, within the body of the airship, off the passageway that ran her full length and allowed access to the engine gondolas, fuel and ballast tanks, and cargo. On the technical side there was one striking advance. While the engines could, if desired, be fed with petrol, they were designed to operate on Blaugas, a gaseous fuel of almost the same weight as air. This meant that the consumption of fuel did not make the *Graf Zeppelin* progressively lighter, and, by corollary, that it was not necessary to release hydrogen in the course of long journeys in order to compensate for such weight loss. As an added bonus Blaugas increased the airship's range by a third.

On 8 July 1928, Count (*Graf*) Zeppelin's birthday, the ship was christened by his daughter, and during the next few weeks a number of trials failed to turn up the slightest imperfection. The maiden flight of 18 September, a thirty-five-hour northern jaunt that took the new ship as far as the east coast of England, was again executed flawlessly. With heady enthusiasm Eckener announced that the *Graf Zeppelin* would arrive in the United States on Columbus Day, 12 October, and that she would be carrying mail and the full complement of twenty passengers.

Unfortunately, the departure, scheduled for the 10th, had to be put off for a day because of bad weather, and even more unfortunate, this bad weather was reported to extend right across the Atlantic in a belt that covered the direct, steamship route that Eckener had planned on. He was tempted by the shorter—but foggy—route that ran in a northern arc from Scotland, but then decided to go the long but presumably safe

way: south to Madeira and then straight across to Bermuda before turning north to Lakehurst. Early on the morning of the 11th, the passengers came aboard, and minutes later they were airborne, moving at full speed west along the Rhine towards the French border. Four officials of the Air Ministry, six newspaper reporters, and the first ten paying passengers ever to cross the Atlantic by air peered through the large observation windows at the Black Forest; then the Saône Valley drifted by below them, the vineyards of Burgundy on the left and the snow-capped Alps on the right; shortly after midday and in sparkling autumn sunshine the *Graf Zeppelin* passed out over the Mediterranean and on towards the Atlantic. Throughout that first day, and the next, which found them far

Opposite: The *Graf Zeppelin* after her christening ceremony (July 1928). Far left: The control cabin of the *Graf Zeppelin* seen through the navigation room (left). Below: The *Graf Zeppelin* coming in to land at the London suburb of Hanworth in August 1931

out over the ocean, flying conditions were ideal, and not even Eckener's uncanny instinct was alerted by the peril that lay ahead. Late on the 12th, radio contact with a station in the Azores, some 250 miles to the north, brought word of an approaching storm; by six in the morning it was upon them with the impact of a brick wall. The nose of the airship pitched violently upward, sending Eckener and the others in the control room spinning backwards towards the door. From behind them came an appalling clatter as kitchen utensils and the recently set breakfast dishes hurtled to the floor. Thunder crashed around them and rain lashed the ship, but the worst of the turbulence was over almost as soon as it began, and with the engines reduced to half throttle Eckener soon had things under control. Indeed he was beginning to congratulate himself and his ship on having weathered the crisis so easily when the Flight Chief brought the alarming report that much of the fabric covering the bottom rear of the port stabilizing fin had been ripped away. The torn remnants were flapping in the wind, dangerously close to the elevator, for if the elevator became jammed the airship would no longer be under control. Eckener reacted with his usual decisiveness. He radioed the U.S. Navy for a relief vessel while he dispatched a small party—which included his son Knut— to cut away the loose fabric. It was an extremely dangerous job because the men had to work exposed to the full force of the slip- stream, but it was completed successfully, and the rest of the journey was gratifyingly uneventful. On the evening of the 15th the *Graf Zeppelin* completed the first of her many Atlantic crossings by landing safely at Lakehurst.

The flight had been front-page news in the United States from the beginning, but events had conspired to make her arrival the occasion of the wildest jubilation. Eckener's prudent request for naval assistance had been followed by several hours of silence, because the airship was travelling too slowly for the propeller- driven generator to provide power for the radio. This ominous quiet was equated with disaster, and banner headlines pro- claimed the death of the mighty airship as a mood of near hysteria gripped the nation. When the *Graf Zeppelin* finally appeared overhead, battered but unbroken, the relief was enormous, the excitement unrestrained. Between twenty and thirty thousand people crowded the Lakehurst airfield, stormed through police cordons protecting the airship, and mobbed the disembarking passengers and crew. For the second time, Eckener found himself to be an American hero, and even his fears that the near disaster might harm the *Graf Zeppelin*'s image proved unfounded. The very fact that she had survived such a mauling at the hands of the elements was taken as proof of her safety, and on this wave of euphoria the return journey got under way two weeks later.

If further proof of the ship's airworthiness was needed the

New York welcomes the crew of the *Graf Zeppelin* with the traditional ticker-tape parade. Eckener is standing up in the front car of the cavalcade

Perhaps the most spectacular view of the *Graf Zeppelin*: soaring over the Alps in 1929. She became not only the most famous airship but virtually synonymous with lighter-than-air travel

eastward flight surely provided it. Eckener decided in favour of the northern route that he had earlier rejected, and after battling heavy squalls most of the way to Newfoundland he ran straight into a blanket of fog. Through the late afternoon the *Graf Zeppelin* flew on, hopefully on course—well south of Newfoundland and heading due east. Then at 5.30 p.m. the ship began to take a savage pounding from the wind, which in itself was not surprising; what astonished Eckener was that he could tell for certain by the violent pitching motion that they were over land. There was not supposed to be any land for two hundred miles! Sure enough, through a small gap in the swirling fog the rocky Newfoundland coast could be seen, and it suddenly dawned on Eckener that southerly winds of enormous velocity, a hurricane in fact, had been steadily driving them farther and farther from their destination. Once he knew where they were in relation to where they were supposed to be, he could calculate the drift at between seventy-five and seventy-six miles per hour. There was no way of fighting that sort of wind and Eckener wisely decided to head north-east, riding with the hurricane until it could eventually be skirted.

Having survived this completely unexpected hazard—the remainder of the flight passed without serious incident— Eckener could draw two simple conclusions. First, his new airship was resilient under the most extreme conditions. Secondly, she was badly underpowered if there was to be any serious attempt to provide a reliable, all-weather Atlantic service. A cruising speed of seventy-odd miles per hour would be derisory in regions where the wind might reach that velocity. The obvious solution was to build a faster ship, which should also be bigger to carry more passengers in greater comfort. But how to raise the money? If Eckener had expected all the favourable publicity attending the *Graf Zeppelin*'s American voyage to loosen official purse-strings he was deluding himself. As before, praise but not money was forthcoming. And he dared not approach the public yet again. The solution, as he saw it, was to dazzle the German nation with a series of prestigious flights, in the hope that sooner or later the weight of public opinion would force the government to relent. The *Graf Zeppelin* was about to enter her most glamorous phase.

The campaign opened with a suggestion to carefully selected government officials and business leaders that they join a luxury cruise. The invitations were picked up with alacrity, and in late March 1929 the *Graf Zeppelin* elegantly roamed the beauty spots of the Mediterranean: from the French Riviera to Corsica; then Rome, the south of Italy, and on to Crete and Cyprus and the eastern shore; Jerusalem, along the coast of Egypt and then north to Athens; up the Adriatic coast and over the Alps to Vienna; and finally through the Danube Valley homeward bound for Friedrichshafen. This spectacular journey lasted

Below: The *Graf Zeppelin* over Lake Constance, where the Zeppelin saga began thirty years before. Right: The airship's spacious and well-appointed dining saloon

eighty-one hours, and at the end of it Eckener could safely count every passenger as a Zeppelin ambassador.

Determined to maintain this momentum Eckener now began talking publicly of the most ambitious enterprise of all: a voyage round the world complete with passengers and mail. With heavy financial backing by the American newspaper czar, William Randolph Hearst, helped by a surge of interest in stamp-collecting quarters—not to mention a ticket price of £1,000—the necessary funds were quickly raised, and Eckener could now devote himself to mapping out a route. The first leg of the journey was determined in advance. Hearst had insisted that the starting point be Lakehurst, so that the flight could begin and end on American soil, and Eckener duly brought the *Graf Zeppelin* across the Atlantic at the beginning of August. This meant that the journey would begin with the return to Friedrichshafen. But for the rest, he faced a bewildering array of choices, for the only landing between Friedrichshafen and Los Angeles was to be Tokyo, and there are many ways to fly from Germany to Japan. After great deliberation Eckener announced that the *Graf Zeppelin* would angle across central Russia and Siberia to a point on the Sea of Okhotsk nearly two thousand miles north of Tokyo, and then run south. This was not

the shortest route but it was the safest, and in many ways the most interesting because the vast reaches of the Siberian interior were a mystery, even to the Russians.

In the early hours of 8 August the great journey got under way, and it began well. The *Graf Zeppelin* swept across the Atlantic with ease, reaching Friedrichshafen in fifty-five hours. Those of the passengers who had not joined the flight at Lakehurst did so now, to complete a most cosmopolitan assortment that included the American airshipman and survivor of the *Shenandoah* disaster, Lieutenant-Commander Rosendahl, the intrepid Hearst reporter, Lady Drummond Hay, Sir Hubert Wilkins, the explorer, and a cantankerous representative of the Soviet government. As they settled back in comfort at dawn on the 15th the airship lifted away from her moorings and struck out north-east for Berlin; from Berlin to Danzig and then on to the Russian border. It was here, at 6 p.m., that Eckener ran into his first difficulty, and it was not the sort of trouble that he was inclined to devote much time or effort to. Moscow lay directly in his intended path, and, not unnaturally, Muscovites were very excited at the prospect of seeing the famous airship over-head. Unhappily, the weather report indicated strong head-winds as far north as Moscow, nothing at all dangerous but

sufficient to slow the ship down and thereby waste some fuel. As always, Eckener put such technical considerations first, and he informed the Soviet representative that they would be altering course so as to avoid the headwinds, and that this would mean they would fly well to the north of Moscow. The Russian was outraged. What about the hundreds of thousands who would be so cruelly disappointed? Purely to save a little fuel? He demanded in the name of the Soviet Government that the *Graf Zeppelin* proceed to Moscow as planned. Eckener bluntly refused and touched off a diplomatic row that could not be patched up until he made a courtesy flight to Moscow the next year.

It was not until the morning, when they were as far north as Vologda, that the airship swung to the east and towards the Urals. Later that day, the 16th, the *Graf Zeppelin* climbed to 3,300 feet and left the mountains—and Europe—behind. From the moment they crossed into Russia the most striking feature of the landscape below was its loneliness, its vast dimensions and sparse settlement, and this impression grew as they moved steadily into the interior. Now, for fourteen unbroken hours, they flew over one of the most desolate regions on earth: a thousand miles of swampland, an enormous watery stretch utterly impassable during summer and locked in an icy strait-jacket for the rest of the year. During its brief summer flowering the area is strikingly beautiful, a jumbled palette of every conceivable hue, but its beauty cannot conceal its terror. To be marooned in such a wasteland is to be lost forever, and as the hours dragged by, almost all daylight hours at this latitude, many of the passengers and crew became visibly uneasy. Finally they reached the Yenisei River, and a settlement of sorts; the tiny, hut-strewn village of Verkne Imbatskoe, whose few inhabitants were plunged into terrible panic as the aerial monster bore down on them.

Taking their bearings once again they made off due east, in the direction of another river, the Tunguska, which they hoped to follow all the way to Yakutsk, on the river Lena in northern Siberia. They also hoped that this route would take them over the site where a great meteorite had smashed into the wilderness twenty-one years before. Photographs of this stupendous natural phenomenon—the flash had been seen 250 miles away and the explosion heard over twice that distance— would have been highly prized. But they had forgotten to check its position before they left, and even their Russian passenger had only a vague idea of the location. They passed by well to the north of the crater, and on towards Yakutsk and the Stanovoi Mountains. Crossing this final hurdle at 6,000 feet and at one point with the jagged rock face a bare 150 feet below her belly, the *Graf Zeppelin* eased out over the Sea of Okhotsk, and into warm sunlight.

Now, on the afternoon of the 18th, Tokyo lay only twenty-four hours to the south, but hasty calculations showed there was enough fuel in hand to go all the way to Los Angeles. Eleven thousand miles non-stop would be an astonishing *tour de force*, but Eckener resisted the temptation. There was not even the excuse of an adverse weather report and he decided, quite rightly, that the Japanese would consider it to be a gratuitous insult to be so brusquely ignored. The *Graf Zeppelin* touched down outside Tokyo the next day, just over 100 hours and 7,000 miles from Friedrichshafen.

Four days later she was on her way across the Pacific, to reach Los Angeles in the early morning of the 26th. And here, with only the comparatively short hop across the United States outstanding, the *Graf Zeppelin* nearly met with disaster. For to descend at Los Angeles it had been necessary to blow off considerable hydrogen because the lower ground temperature (the phenomenon of temperature inversion) made the ship too buoyant. The cells were refilled, but during the afternoon hot sunshine caused the gas to expand, with the result that more

The *Graf Zeppelin* skirting St Paul's Cathedral during her tour of Britain in 1931. During her lifetime this most successful of airships flew more than a million miles

was automatically released to maintain the correct pressure. When they came to take off the ship would not budge. She was far too heavy, and there was no hydrogen left to replenish the cells. Eckener promptly dispatched some of the crew to Lakehurst by train, pared fuel and ballast to the bone, and ordered take-off. The airship duly rose in the cool ground air, but the moment she entered the markedly warmer air lying just above ground level she was once again too heavy. There was only one way out, and that was to speed along, almost touching the ground, with the nose slightly inclined so as to force a path slowly up into the warmer air. This was attempted and it appeared to be working, if painfully slowly. Then suddenly high-tension wires appeared directly in front at a height of sixty-five feet. It was too late to stop, and to hit them would be catastrophic; it would mean annihilation. Eckener instantly applied maximum elevator to get the nose up over the wires, and as he did so the tail raked the ground. The wires passed beneath the control car but they were right in the path of the stern, which was still dragging. At the very last moment Eckener gave the order 'Down elevator'. The nose pitched forward and the tail flipped over the deadly wires. Eckener, who later admitted that he was badly shaken by the experience, estimated that the clearance was three feet. The *Graf Zeppelin* never came closer to destruction.

Lakehurst, another ticker-tape parade through New York, and the triumph was complete. But while it was impossible to stage a more impressive demonstration of the *Graf Zeppelin*'s capabilities than this round-the-world voyage, Eckener realized that it was essential to keep flying, to keep his only airship before the public eye in order to drum up—from any quarter—the only sort of interest that could make his dream of another ship, indeed a fleet of ships, come true: financial interest. In 1930 the

Graf Zeppelin crossed the south Atlantic to Brazil, the beginning of a long and profitable association with the South American continent. In 1931 she carried a scientific expedition on an extensive survey of the Arctic, and did so with remarkable ease. In 1932 the regular service to South America got into full swing. The thirties, Eckener was confident, would be the decade of the Zeppelin.

Over these past few years, however, Germany's airship supremacy had not gone unchallenged, and the last of her competitors, the U.S. Navy, would not bow out for some time to come. As early as 1924, after thoroughly digesting the implications of the *R38* disaster, the British government had decided that the interests of a far-flung empire could be served ideally by large passenger airships. Accordingly, a major construction programme was launched, and this time there would be no simple copying of an existing Zeppelin. Furthermore, two airships would be built simultaneously, one by the Vickers-owned Airship Guarantee Company and the other by the Air Ministry itself. They would be the largest, most sophisticated airships ever built—much larger, in fact, than the future *Graf Zeppelin*—capable of transporting 100 passengers in speed and comfort over great distances. The last disastrous chapter in Britain's airship history had opened.

The Vickers airship, designated *R100*, was quietly put together over a period of five years at the disused hangar at Howden. Designed by the formidable Barnes Wallis and assembled by a skilled staff that included the young Neville Shute Norway, the airship emerged for her opening trials in November 1929. The few technical snags that showed up in these trials could not disguise that fact that Wallis and his men had constructed a first-rate airship, perhaps as good as the *Graf Zeppelin* and also much larger and considerably faster.

During the same five-year period the government team, working at Cardington, and under the scrutiny of almost continuous publicity, produced an equally large and much better-looking airship that can fairly be described as bad in conception, bungled in construction, and in the final analysis nothing more that a grotesque tribute to official stupidity: the much bally-hooed *R101*.

To begin with, despite the obvious advantages of pooling information with the designers at Howden, a collaboration that Wallis repeatedly suggested, the Cardington team behaved as though it were too proud to learn from its rival's mistakes. That was a pity because it showed an astonishing inability to learn from its own, and they were legion. One can begin almost anywhere. The new diesel engines were far too heavy, and blatantly so. Perhaps because so much publicity had been given to their supposed superiority when they were designed (there was a marginal safety factor in their favour) it was considered

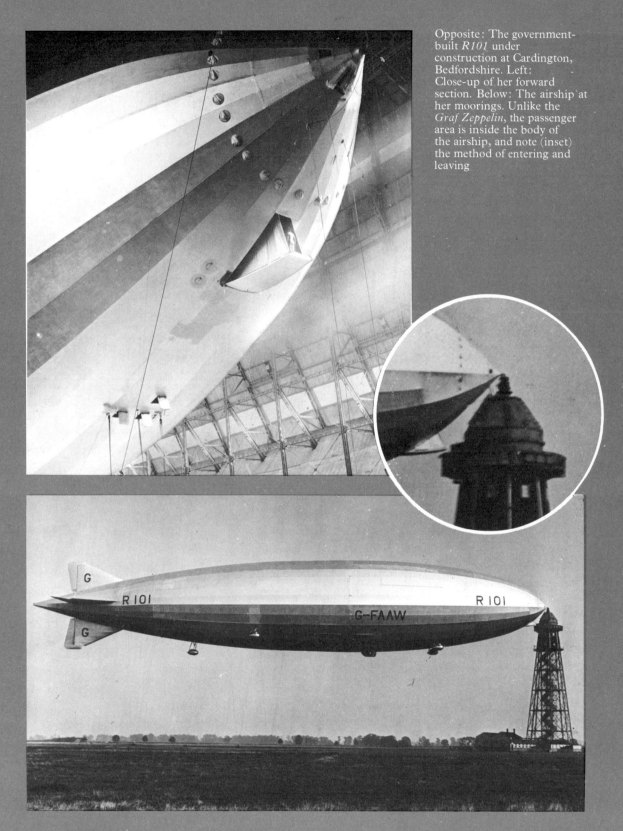

Opposite: The government-built *R101* under construction at Cardington, Bedfordshire. Left: Close-up of her forward section. Below: The airship at her moorings. Unlike the *Graf Zeppelin*, the passenger area is inside the body of the airship, and note (inset) the method of entering and leaving

The dining saloon of the
ill-fated *R101*. From there, on
the evening of 4 October
1930, the passengers retired
'after an excellent supper'

impossible to scrap them and revert to conventional gasoline
engines, like the Rolls-Royce Condor engines installed in *R100*.
In any case the diesel engines stayed. The gasbags were wired
into the framework in such a way that they chafed against the
many projections that formed an integral part of the surrounding
structure. If that were not bad enough, when the ship rolled—
which she was very prone to do—the valves opened slightly,
allowing gas to escape.

These crucial faults showed up as soon as the test flights began
in October 1929. Not only were the engines so heavy as to
critically affect lifting power, they were subject to chronic
breakdown. It was noted that jagged holes appeared in the
gasbags after the airship had been moored outside in a stiff wind.
At the same time the malfunction of the valves was reported.
The way in which these problems were tackled was typical of the
entire venture. In order to increase the lift the airship was
chopped in two and an additional bay inserted in the middle.
Then some of the accommodation fittings were ripped out and
the existing gasbag wiring loosened to allow for greater
expansion—and greater chafing. The offending projections were
padded. The valves were hopefully repaired. The results of this
'scissors and paste' approach were even worse than might be
expected. No sooner was the new *R101* dragged out to her
mooring-mast than a horrifying split opened up along the top of
the envelope. It was taped up. The next day another smaller
split appeared. It too was taped.

All this was done in great haste because of sustained and
mounting pressure that the ship be made ready at once. Both
R100 and *R101* were committed to a conspicuous inauguration,
the former earmarked for a transatlantic flight to Canada and the
latter for an even longer voyage to India. At the end of July 1930,

R100 duly set off for Montreal, managed the flight easily, and returned two weeks later. Why was *R101* not ready? Worse, it was rumoured that the deepening economic crisis would result in one of the two ships being scrapped. If that were so it would obviously be the more successful of the two that was kept, and at the moment there was no question which that was. The India flight had to be made, and quickly. The final nail in the *R101*'s coffin was provided by the Air Minister himself, Lord Thomson. He had commitments to fulfil in India in September and he blithely announced his intention of getting there by airship. And he would get there on time, because 'I have made my plans accordingly.'

September was utterly impossible, and while Thomson eventually bowed to the delay he did so with bad grace. He fully expected to be the next Viceroy of India, and nothing was going to interfere with his grandly conceived arrival in the subcontinent. Therefore he rearranged his meetings for October, and informed the *R101* team that the departure would be on the 4th of that month. He could not be brooked again, and work continued round the clock in a desperate effort to make the best of a bad job. A few trials were carried out but nothing sufficient to warrant the issuing of a Certificate of Airworthiness, mandatory for the flight; but this problem, like all the others, could be side-stepped neatly. A temporary certificate was issued with the question-begging proviso that the final speed trials be completed during the journey. The most charitable interpretation that can be put on such double-think is that it stemmed from gross incompetence.

So it was that at 6.36 p.m. on 4 October, the airship that was, in Thomson's words, 'as safe as a house, except for the millionth chance', rose sluggishly from Cardington and set a course for the English Channel; just to get her into the air it had been necessary to jettison nearly half the water ballast. Three hours later she was over Hastings, with one engine out of commission, battling wind and rain and with a forecast of worse weather ahead. At 11.26 she laboured over the French coast near Dieppe, and the six passengers retired for the evening, 'after an excellent supper'. *R101* now had less than three hours to survive.

As she moved deeper into Normandy, slowly against the wind, those on the ground who saw her were struck by what seemed the foolhardy policy of flying at very low altitude—at one point estimated to be no more than 300 feet. They could not know that it was not by choice. Just after 2 a.m., over the small town of Beauvais, the dying airship pitched forward, corrected herself when the emergency ballast was hastily released, and then slowly glided into the side of a hill and came to rest, completely intact. A moment later there was a ghastly explosion and *R101* became an inferno. Only six of the fifty-four aboard came out alive, and Lord Thomson was not among them.

The skeletal framework of
R101 stands out in macabre
relief against the Normandy
hillside. Above: Crowds
gather around the wreckage.
Right: Members of the public
file past victims of the
holocaust, lying in state in
Westminster Hall, London

The *Akron* in flight (below) and under construction (opposite). In April 1933 she plunged into the Atlantic, killing seventy-four—the heaviest toll for any airship disaster

Overleaf: The mighty *Hindenburg* over Manhattan on her final flight

The *R101* disaster put an instant finish to British efforts with rigid airships, and the guiltless *R100* was sold for scrap, for £450. The field was now reduced to Germany and the United States.

America entered the thirties with only one rigid airship, the sturdy, German-built *Los Angeles*, but the Goodyear Tire and Rubber Company was forging ahead with the construction of a gigantic new airship, the *Akron*, and this was to be followed by a sister ship, the *Macon*. Completed by the summer of 1931, the *Akron's* most startling feature aside from her massive dimensions was an actual hangar, sunk into the belly of the airship and from which as many as five small aeroplanes could be launched during flight. This ingenious modification worked well, as did everything about the splendid new ship. But the jinx that had destroyed so many other good airships, and would later destroy the finest of all, eventually caught up with her. On the night of 4–5 April 1933 she plunged into the Atlantic during a severe storm. The crash was attributed to pilot error, not structural failure, but the loss of seventy-three men, the heaviest toll ever

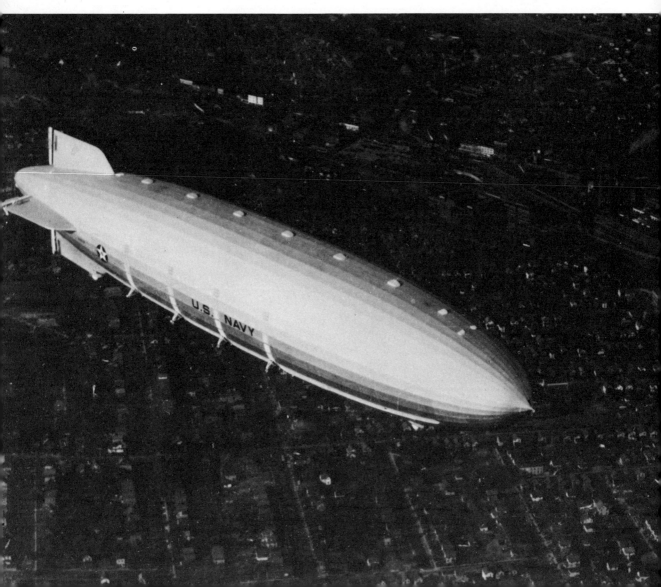

in an airship disaster, greatly increased doubts about the soundness of the entire concept. Then just under two years later, in February 1935, the *Macon* ditched in the Pacific. All but two of the eighty-three aboard survived, but the navy's rigid airship programme did not. And that meant that with the *Los Angeles* long out of service the *Graf Zeppelin* was the only rigid airship still flying anywhere in the world.

The solitary status of the *Graf Zeppelin* was something that Eckener had already taken steps to alter, although the eventual success of his long campaign to get government backing for a new airship heralded his eclipse as master of the Zeppelin fortunes. When the Nazis came to power in January 1933 they viewed Eckener and his airship plans with mixed feelings. On the one hand a great many Germans (and outsiders) had seen the venerable airshipman as a natural successor to Hindenburg as president, and while Eckener appeared immune to such blandishments, the new regime could not view with equanimity even a potential rival, especially one with such widespread

popularity. Somehow this national hero must be cut down to size. As for airships as such, Hitler had no time for them, and Goering, an aeroplane enthusiast, was lukewarm at best; the airship was of no military value. On the other hand, that enormous prestige accrued to Germany as a result of the *Graf Zeppelin*'s marathon exploits was undeniable. And Joseph Goebbels was not slow to recognize the value of such ready-made propaganda. Moreover, if the Zeppelin organization was not exactly affluent, it was managing to hold its own solely on the strength of the *Graf Zeppelin*'s South American service. It could easily be demonstrated that by doubling the size of this fleet of one, and thereby opening a north as well as south Atlantic service, the operation would turn a nice profit.

109

The obvious solution to this thorny problem was to bring the Zeppelin programme under state control, and in March 1935 Goering himself presided over the founding of the German Zeppelin Airline Company, superficially a well-heeled extension of the old Zeppelin Company, but a concern in which the government-backed Lufthansa airline held half the shares. In one respect Eckener had to welcome the move, for the immediate injection of funds meant that work could proceed confidently on his dream airship. It also meant that Eckener was straightaway 'promoted' out of harm's way to the board of directors, and that actual flight operations would never again be under his iron control.

This critical turn of events in the mid thirties ushered in the last, ultimately tragic phase of the Zeppelin saga. The new airship, named *Hindenburg* even before she left the drawing boards, was ready by March 1936. This was the end product of nearly forty years of Zeppelin engineering skill. While only marginally longer than the *Graf Zeppelin*, her capacity of seven million cubic feet was nearly twice as great, while four massive diesel engines churned out 1,100 horsepower each, giving a cruising speed of just under eighty miles per hour. But it was not so much the external dimensions or the brute power of the *Hindenburg* that made her different in kind from all previous airships. Within her massive bulk, and because of it, Eckener and his designers had been able to realize the ideal of a passenger airship that made no compromises to its mode of travel: the *Hindenburg* was expressly designed to provide the standard of comfort and luxury that could be obtained on a transatlantic liner. The twenty-five two-berth cabins were electrically heated and equipped with hot and cold running water. On one side of the principal corridor lay a spacious dining-room, served by a modern, electric galley, while on the other side was a saloon and separate reading-and-writing room. Between meal times passengers could stretch out in light-weight but tasteful furniture, and amuse themselves with a baby grand piano—made of aluminium and weighing but 112 pounds. Or they could stroll down either side of the promenade deck and enjoy an unimpeded view of the world beneath, through massive observation windows that inclined steeply outwards. And that en route to the real luxury aboard: a bar and smoking-room. For despite the proximity of seven million cubic feet of inflammable hydrogen, the Zeppelin engineers had constructed a foolproof method by which passengers could safely smoke. The room was sealed by double doors and kept at a higher pressure than the rest of the ship, so that it was impossible for hydrogen, should it somehow escape, to drift inside. And to remove the danger of human carelessness, passengers had to hand over all cigarette lighters and matches on boarding, and the lighters in the smoking-room were chained down.

Far left: The *Hindenburg* over Berlin's Brandenburg Gate. Left: Passengers dining aboard the *Hindenburg* in October 1936; Eckener is arrowed. The largest airship ever built, she was also the most luxurious—right down to a baby grand piano

The *Hindenburg* at Lakehurst in May 1936. Her considerably older sister, the *Los Angeles* (no longer in service), can be seen in the background

In one important respect, however, the *Hindenburg* was not as her designers wished. Like all the earlier Zeppelins she was inflated with hydrogen, and despite the U.S. Navy's grim record with helium-filled airships no one seriously doubted that the loss of buoyancy with this heavier, non-flammable gas was vastly outweighed by the safety factor. Eckener repeatedly used his good offices with Roosevelt to try to lift an embargo on the export of helium (America alone possessed the gas in quantity). He finally succeeded—shortly after the *Hindenburg*'s last flight.

In May 1936, after one flight to South America, the new Zeppelin took her appointed place on the regular Lakehurst run, and during the remainder of that year she completed ten round trips (Frankfurt was now the German terminus). She also managed six more crossings to Rio de Janeiro, and so great was the demand for her services that when she was layed up for the winter months, twenty more cabins were installed. At the same time the ageing *Graf Zeppelin* was continuing to ferry passengers between Germany and Brazil with unfailing regularity. It is worth pausing to reflect on her lifetime performance by the end of that 1936 season: in eight years she had flown nearly six hundred times, covered more than a million miles, and carried nearly thirteen thousand passengers. Both the South and North American services were to be increased the next year. With the *Graf Zeppelin* taking the bulk of the load, there were to be twenty crossings to Brazil, while the *Hindenburg* herself would make eighteen journeys to Lakehurst. And work was proceeding on yet another Zeppelin, very similar to the *Hindenburg* yet bearing the name *Graf Zeppelin II*.

So even if relations between Eckener and the Nazis were getting steadily worse, and the Americans still refused to part with helium, and a spate of sabotage threats provided a grim reminder of how unpopular Germany and all things German were becoming: even so the Zeppelin enterprise, dogged all its life by bad luck, was poised for the stable commercial success that had proved so elusive. And if everyone else was quitting the field, so much the better. Not that there had ever been any serious competition, but those sensational disasters did great harm to public confidence in airships, a confidence that the Zeppelin had fought hard for and completely warranted. After all, Zeppelins never crashed. From the inception of DELAG's passenger service in 1910, more than fifty thousand people had reached their destinations safely; no one had received the slightest injury.

That was how the record stood at 7.25 p.m. on 6 May 1937, as the *Graf Zeppelin* droned steadily closer to the Mediterranean, two days out from Brazil, and the *Hindenburg* hovered a hundred feet or so above the airfield at Lakehurst, the mooring ropes already in the hands of the ground crew, and the first crossing of the new season moments from completion. The *Graf Zeppelin*, near the Canary Islands, had just received a radio message from the *Hindenburg* announcing her safe arrival at Lakehurst.

Sabotage? Static electricity? An Act of God? One moment the mighty *Hindenburg* was there. The next moment she was gone. No one who has heard the oft-repeated radio commentary by Herb Morrison can ever forget his anguished cry: 'It's broken into flames! It's flashing—flashing! It's flashing terribly! It's bursting into flames . . .' Those aboard were the last to know that they had been overwhelmed by calamity. Some heard a slight popping sound coming from the direction of the stern. Others, gazing through the observation windows, saw the sudden horror written on the faces below. A burst of flame from the stern, and then the entire sky was alight. The tail sank towards the ground, shattered; girders screamed, snapped— and, above all, the terrible whoosh of flames, the continuous explosion as seven million cubic feet of hydrogen, a sixth of a mile of airship, became a blazing torch.

As the flames swept forward, engulfing cell after cell, the airship dropped, slowly, and disintegrated. Through and around the blistering flames people were running, spectators, ground crew, and, incredibly, passengers and crew from the *Hindenburg*. Thirty-two seconds had elapsed since the initial explosion, and in that half-minute the passenger airship had vanished forever.

THE WEATHER
Today: Fair, little change in
temperature
morrow: Fair, little change in
temperature
mperatures yesterday: Max., 71; Min., 54
Detailed Report on Page 35

Herald

FRIDAY, M

(Copyright, 1937,
New York Tribune Inc.)

VOL. XCVII No. 33,015

Hindenburg Explode
Dirigible, Landing, F

Horror Dazes Field Crowd Unable to Aid

Allen, Herald Tribune Aviation Editor, Pictures Spectacle He Sees as 'Most Terrible' of Air

Storms Kept Ship Drifting 3 Hours

Air Station a Madhouse of Activity as Trucks and Ambulances Race Out to Succor Victims

By C. B. Allen

Herald Tribune Aviation Editor

LAKEHURST, N. J., May 6.—Spectators peering through the light rain at the ground crew walking the Hindenburg to her mooring mast at the air field here tonight froze silent and then cried out in horror when they saw flames flare out from the hulk of the giant airship on the starboard side, a third the way forward from the tail, and spread in a great burst down the length of the ship.

Most of them had waited wearily at the field from the time, 4:15 p. m., when the Hindenburg was first sighted from the Naval Air Station. Through a gusty wind and unsuitable landing conditions the big ship weld evidently pre-

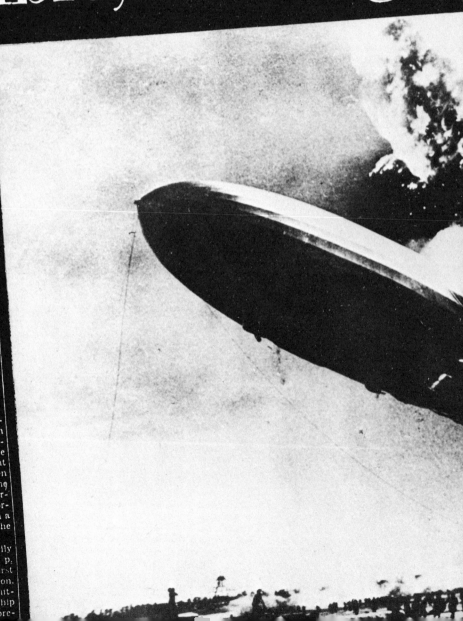

at Lakehurst, 34 Die;
lls 500 Feet in Flames

63 Survive in Plunge
Of Burning Zeppeli

World's Largest Airship Shattered
She Approaches Mooring Mast a
End of Season's First Flight

Static Electricity Theor
Is Advanced as a Cau

Commander Pruss and Captain Lehmann S
Latter Believed Dying; Ground Crew in Per
Heat Drives Rescuers Back From Shi

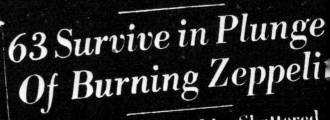

The German dirigible Hindenburg, largest airship ever bu
destroyed by explosions and fire at 7:23 o'clock last nigh
swing toward her mooring mast at the Naval Air Station, L
N. J. Thirty-four of the ninety-seven persons aboard wer
to have lost their lives in the crash of the great airliner. T
the thirty-six passengers and forty-three of the sixty-one
members of the crew escaped.

Of the survivors, however, many are expected to die
as the foot dirigible fell to earth in flu
seconds from the scheduled end of her first 1937 cross
United St

Among these is Captain Ernst A. Lehmann, former com
the Hindenburg, who served in an advisory capacity on the
round-trip crossings scheduled for this yea
third-degree burns, he received the last rites of
tholic Church in Paul Kimball Hospital, Lakewood, and
a German interpreter, to whom he dictated his will. C
Pruss, commander of the airliner, also is in Paul Kimball
less seriously injured.

The Hindenburg, which sailed from Frankfort, G
Monday night, was destroyed on the first anniversary of h
on her first voyag
America from Germa
Four hours before h

Zeppelin Dead

Previous pages (116–121):
The *Hindenburg*'s final
moments at Lakehurst, 6 May
1937: the airship bursts into
flames at 7.25 p.m.; moments
later she disintegrates on the
landing field

Above: Eckener arrives at the
Vienna aerodrome to fly to
Berlin, en route to New York
and the official inquiry into
the tragedy. Whatever caused
it, this final catastrophe
marked the eclipse of the
passenger airship

Ninety-seven people had boarded the *Hindenburg* at Frankfurt; thirty-five of them died at Lakehurst along with one
member of the ground crew. Of that total thirteen were
passengers. The crew victims included Ernst Lehmann,
Eckener's successor as operations chief, who managed to stagger
clear of the wreckage but died within hours from the burns he
sustained. To the modern mind, which has had to come to
terms with the appalling carnage of aeroplane disasters, the fact
that so many people came out alive reduces the tragedy to
manageable proportions. Jet crashes are rarely selective. Yet in
the 'hierarchy' of travel disasters the *Hindenburg* is matched only
by the *Titanic* in the deep, universal feeling of awe and horror
that it inspired, and inspires still; and in both cases the name
itself implies the disaster. There are interesting parallels between
the two. Each vessel was immense, the largest of its kind; each
was the best, the very finest product of a tradition and skill that
was unrivalled; each was surrounded by an aura of invincibility;
each died young, and at a time when omens of impending doom
would later take on a significance. The great difference is that
the sinking of the *Titanic* did not spell the end of the passenger
steamship.

Rumours of sabotage sprang up at once, and even Eckener's
immediate reaction was that foul play was at least likely. But
the Board of Inquiry, on which Eckener was represented, came
up with an entirely different explanation, one that he put forward
himself after sifting the evidence. A thunderstorm had passed

over Lakehurst just before the attempted landing, and another squall was approaching. This meant that there had been considerable differences in electrical potential all around the airship, and perhaps lightning as well. This in itself was not uncommon, and hydrogen-filled airships had landed in such conditions countless times. Even direct hits by lightning were not considered too serious, as the metal framework could absorb the charge. But some observers had noticed a small flame, recognizably pure hydrogen, playing near the stern moments before the first explosion, and this meant that gas had escaped from one of the cells. This finding was corroborated by the demonstrable fact that throughout the landing manoeuvres the *Hindenburg* had been stern heavy, and corrective measures had failed to bring the ship level. A considerable loss of gas from one of the rear cells would account for this. How the leak occurred could only be supposed, but the tricky wind conditions had necessitated a sharp turn during the approach, and a bracing wire might have snapped under the strain and pierced the cell. What ignited the free hydrogen was also guesswork, but under such atmospheric conditions a brush discharge could occur only too easily. Once the pure hydrogen was alight the ship was lost: as soon as the flame reached a point where the slow-burning hydrogen was mixing with air an explosion was certain.

Despite the weight of evidence to suggest that the *Hindenburg* was the victim of a freak combination of circumstances, the more dramatically satisfying explanation of sabotage proved, and still proves, impossible to lay to rest. The best evidence to support it is that there were certainly groups and individuals who hated the swastika-emblazoned airship and everything it stood for enough to destroy it. In any case they would be tormented by this particular symbol of German might no more. The *Graf Zeppelin* was taken out of service at once, initially as a temporary measure until the findings on the Lakehurst disaster were completed. The *Graf Zeppelin II* was ready by September 1938, but the helium earmarked for her never arrived. Hitler's takeover of Austria six months earlier had finally and irrevocably hardened America's attitude. Inflated with hydrogen, the magnificent new airship made a few trial flights the following year, and then was broken up soon after the war started; at the same time work ground to a halt on yet another, even larger Zeppelin. The *Graf Zeppelin II*'s aluminium framework disappeared into the anonymity of fighter aeroplanes, and despite pleas that the old *Graf Zeppelin* be spared, even as a museum piece, she too was cannibalized for Goering's *Luftwaffe*. This was March 1940. On 6 May, three years to the day after the *Hindenburg* calamity, the great hangars at Frankfurt were blown up to make more room for aeroplanes. It was an accurate, if brutal, comment on the totality of the aeroplane's victory over its old rival.

6 POSTSCRIPT TO AN ERA

IN a sense the *Hindenburg* disaster, and the world disaster that swept up the German airship industry in its wake, is the bitter conclusion to the age of the airship. No one under middle age can remember seeing one of the great monarchs of the sky, and the rare appearance of an advertising blimp summons up much the same feeling that a fully rigged clipper ship on the high seas would evoke: nostalgia, a brief glimpse into the past, and in the case of airships just an inkling of how stupendous the real thing must have been. For an advertising blimp is a pale shadow of a passenger airship. Yet there is a sequel, prosaic though it may seem beside the glories that were and might have been.

While the U.S. Navy abandoned rigid airships after the *Macon* came to grief in 1935, it did not apply a similar policy to non-rigid airships, or blimps as they were called. Goodyear, who built the blimps for the navy, also employed them for advertising and for carrying passengers. While they did not establish a regular service, or attempt great distances, Goodyear blimps enjoyed an unblemished safety record while carrying several hundred thousand passengers on short hops.

When war broke out in Europe in 1939, and as the likelihood of American involvement grew, the U.S. Navy began in earnest to assemble a large fleet of blimps for patrol duties, a function which they had performed so well during the First World War. In this second and greater test, the humble blimp again covered itself with glory. The most important task allocated to the airship squadrons was convoy patrol, and in the entire course of the war not one ship guarded by blimps was lost. Their versatility was astonishing. They could operate in weather conditions that grounded other aircraft, refuel and exchange crews from aircraft carriers, stay airborne for days on end.

The navy blimps did not go out with the war, although their numbers were greatly reduced. New and improved types appeared during the late forties and throughout the fifties, eventually filling a vital role in the early-warning radar system. But even here, where its qualities of endurance, dependability, and enormous range might have ensured it a permanent future, the aeroplane, linked to an expanding network of radar stations, soon rendered the blimp obsolete. The construction programmes lapsed, de-commissioned blimps were not replaced, and the remaining few were phased out in the early 1960s.

Having finally lost their great customer, Goodyear had either to give up airships altogether, or else to concentrate exclusively on commercial blimps. They chose the latter, and for that reason the blimp is still occasionally in evidence, almost invariably linked with some advertising campaign or other. But advertising need not be its sole function: the British-owned *Europa*, repaired after being severely damaged in April 1972, provides an ideal platform for aerial surveys and for televizing certain outside

Left: A U.S. Navy blimp developed for anti-submarine patrols during the Second World War. These blimps gave superb protection to convoys

Overleaf: The *Europa*, a modern blimp built by Goodyear and based in England. While her main purpose is for advertising, the *Europa* is ideal for television coverage of outdoor events

sporting events, such as motor races. Still, it seems a trivial, even shabby finale to a noble dream.

Can the airship expect better from the future? Any proposal for its revival as a serious concern, in other words for transporting goods or passengers, must face severe, perhaps crippling opposition; not just from the aeroplane industry, with its vested interest in the matter, but from a highly sceptical public. It is generally believed that the airship, any airship, is inherently unsafe. It is an attractive idea, romantic even, but it is fundamentally whimsical, backward-looking, unprogressive. The airship had its chance and it was a demonstrable failure. It may be a pity, but progress is unsentimental. This view clearly must be shaken if any of the ambitious schemes afoot are to stand a chance, although it would seem that this could only be done by a sustained success, and that can hardly occur without a major commitment. Who is prepared to try? And why should they?

The Aereon Corporation, launched in the United States in the mid sixties, ran short of money after making a small prototype of a proposed 150 m.p.h. diesel-powered airship. Since then they have been studying the possibility of an imaginative blend of lighter-than-air and heavier-than-air principles; a craft looking vaguely like a delta-wing aeroplane, filled with helium and powered by turbo-prop engines. If successful it would be economical for long-distance cargo operations. In fact the shifting of cargo, not passengers, is the keynote of the revival of interest in airships in several countries, including Germany and the Soviet Union. In Britain there are two private concerns, Cargo Airships Ltd (a subsidiary of Manchester Liners) and Airfloat Transport Ltd, examining the feasibility of lighter-than-air transport. Cargo Airships plans to go ahead with a small prototype, although the project as conceived is anything but small. What is envisaged is a rigid airship of some thirty million cubic foot capacity, nearly a quarter of a mile in length. In marked contrast to airships of the past, this would have an outer shell designed to take the stresses that in Zeppelin-type airships fell on the skeleton framework. An operational speed of 100 miles per hour is projected, at least in the first instance and with diesel engines, but were nuclear power employed the speed could double.

The case for the cargo airship is impressive. Aeroplanes have managed only to skim the surface of this enormous industry because the cost-to-weight ratio is prohibitive in almost all cases. So it is that we approach the last quarter of the twentieth century with substantially the same methods of conveying goods over long distances with which we entered the first quarter: rail (or road, but wheeled in any case), and steamship. In that context, the airship is not backward-looking; it could be a striking advance, in harmony with the move towards containerization.

Some of the advantages that a large cargo airship would

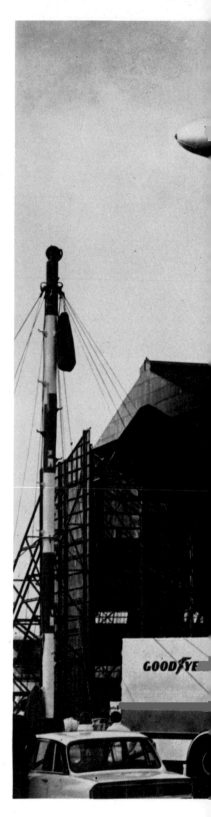

enjoy appear overwhelming. One hundred miles per hour—without delays along the way—means twenty-four hundred miles in a day. Equipped with its own hoisting apparatus, perhaps even with straddle helicopters, the airship could load containers at the point of manufacture, and deliver direct to the customer, anywhere in the world. It would not even need a landing field. What this could mean for the development of remote or industrially backward areas is inestimable. Moreover, as demonstrated time and again by blimps, an advanced airship would be able to operate in conditions that aeroplanes could never attempt. Finally, and this cannot be stressed too heavily, a helium-filled airship, constructed in the light of current knowledge of aerodynamics, stress factors, and metal fatigue, guided by the wealth of meteorological data that is now available (such information doubtless assimilated by computers on board), really would be 'as safe as a house', and there might not even be the millionth chance.

So what about passenger airships? If the prospect here is far less likely than with cargo airships, it is no less exciting. Suppose cargo airships were to succeed dramatically, and were seen to be safe as well as profitable? Would the passenger airship become a serious proposition? If 200 miles per hour is taken as an outside (and very optimistic) figure, it is unlikely in the extreme that the airship, no matter how much it could offer in the way of comfort and safety, could make much of an impression on a public geared to jet travel. After all, the decision to go ahead with supersonic transport in the face of staggering costs is based on the assumption that when the faster is available the slower becomes bothersome; if past experience is anything to go by it is a reasonable assumption. On the other hand, the idea of actually *touring* by airship (again, provided there were confidence in its safety) is exciting to say the least. There is no reason why the standard of accommodation should not rival that of a five-star hotel—or a cut-price holiday centre if that were the intended market. In every other respect the airship would be peerless. It would be quiet, if nuclear-powered utterly silent. Airsickness is almost unknown on airships. It could fly low, slowly, over parts of the world inaccessible by other means. It could stop, to hover motionless a few hundred feet above—what? The North Pole? The Himalayas? The heart of the Amazon basin? What could rival such a journey over African wildlife preserves?

The vision may be quixotic, in part or in whole, and we may have to settle for unexciting little advertising blimps. But to those who are restive about clogged motorways and barbarous public transport, about pollution and noise and environmental mayhem, about the unsettling jolt from airport to airport and the general lack of graciousness in contemporary travel; to those people the airship is worth a second, or maybe a first glance.

Photo acknowledgments

E. C. P. Armées: 56 (right)

Associated Press: 76, 80, 84–85, 118, 122

Beringer & Pampaluchi: 95

British Museum (Reproduced by courtesy of the Trustees): 14

Cargo Airships Ltd: back endpapers

Conway Picture Library: 53 (btm), 54–55, 66–67, 71, 72, 91 (btm), 102, 104

F. A. Dinsdale: 53 (top)

Flight International: front endpapers, 36–37 (btm), 56 (left), 58–59, 68–69, 100, 103, 109 (right)

Goodyear: 79,

Imperial War Museum: 37 (top), 48, 56–57, 60

Mary Evans Picture Library: 8–9, 13, 16–17, 18, 45 (right)

Press Association: 30, 70, 88–89, 99, 106 (top), 107 (top)

Radio Times Hulton Picture Library: 6–7, 21, 22–23, 40–41, 44–45 (centre), 47, 52–53 (btm), 62–63, 74, 83

J. Reed: 52 (top)

Robert Hunt Library: 4–5, 43, 44 (btm), 49, 51, 58 (top), 59 (top)

M. Rol & Cie: 36 (top)

Royal Aeronautical Society: 2–3, 38–39, 65, 90, 91 (top), 108, 124

Saga Services Ltd: 126–127

Syndications International: 106–107

Ullstein Bilderdienst: 26–27, 29, 31, 32–33, 34–35, 87, 97, 110–111, 112 (top), 114

United Press International: 92–93, 112–113, 116–117, 119, 120–121

William Gordon Davies: 10–11, 22, 44 (left), 96

Front cover: Beringer & Pampaluchi

Back cover: Conway Picture Library, Mary Evans Picture Library, Radio Times Hulton Picture Library, *Sunday Express*, Ullstein Bilderdienst, United Press International

Back end papers: Produced for Cargo Airships Ltd, this drawing shows some of the possible features of an airship of the future

128